Desert Spirituality for Men

Desert Spirituality for Men

BRAD KARELIUS

Foreword by Eileen McNerney, CSJ

RESOURCE *Publications* · Eugene, Oregon

DESERT SPIRITUALITY FOR MEN

Resource Publications
An Imprint of Wipf and Stock Publishers
199 W. 8th Ave., Suite 3
Eugene, OR 97401

www.wipfandstock.com

PAPERBACK ISBN: 978-1-6667-3315-0
HARDCOVER ISBN: 978-1-6667-2752-4
EBOOK ISBN: 978-1-6667-2753-1

VERSION NUMBER 060922

This book is written with gratitude
for the Sisters of Saint Joseph of Orange,
partners in ministry for forty years:1981–2021.

Contents

Permissions

AN EARLIER VERSION OF Chapter Seventeen appeared as "Home is Right Here" in the Jesuit magazine, America. Reprinted with permission of America Press, Inc., americamagazine.org.

A different version of Chapter Five appeared as "A Trip to East Germany," in, The Living Church.

Whitney Hopler, quotations from Saint Francis of Assisi and His Sermon to the Birds, from Learn Religions, August 27, 2020, an online resource. Used with permission of Dotdash Publishing.

Philip Kosloski, quotations from, A Beginner's Guide to Praying the Liturgy of the Hours, an online resource. Used with permission from the author.

Verse 11, Chapter 13, Book I from, Ascent of Mount Carmel by Saint John of the Cross, translated by Kieran Kavanaugh ©1987. Used by permission of SPCK Publishing, London, United Kingdom.

Brief quotations from pp. 46–47, 190 (stand alone) of The Wisdom of the Wilderness: Experiencing the Healing Power of Nature, by Gerald G. May, copyright ©2006. Used by permission of Harper Collins Publishers.

Quotations from *The Book of Common Prayer*, the Church Hymnal Corporation, ©1979. Used by permission. All rights reserved worldwide.

Scripture quotations taken from *The Holy Bible, New International Version*®, NIV®. Copyright © 1973, 1978, 1984, 2011 by Biblica, Inc.®. Used by permission. All rights reserved worldwide.

Thank you to Giles Brown Literary Agency for permission in the United Kingdom and British Commonwealth excluding Canada to quote from *The Wisdom of Wilderness: Experiencing the Healing Power of Nature* by

Foreword

WE LIVE OUR LIVES forward, but we understand them backwards. That's what Brad Karelius was doing when he sat down to write *Desert Spirituality for Men*.

Henri Nouwen, a priest whose spirituality was deeply embedded in psychology, noted that, "to write is to embark on a journey that we do not know." He said that, "writing is an act of trust. It's like giving away the few loaves and fishes that one has and trusting that they will multiply in the giving." Nouwen reminded his readers that, "once we dare to give away on paper the few thoughts that come to us, that we then start discovering how much is hidden underneath these thoughts and gradually come in touch with our own riches."[1]

By first remembering and then exploring his life story, Brad candidly sets before us a number of paths that he has taken in life to find both God and himself. Imbued by his creator with a great curiosity about the world, about people, about cultures, about nature, about faith, and about life itself, Brad has sought to find God everywhere—even along the uneven paths and rocky trails of his life.

As an Episcopal priest, Brad has long desired to be a man of God, a man strong and humble enough that God could trust him and use him to bring God to people, and people to God in circumstances that he might never have imagined.

With humble candor, Brad refers to an incident on his way to adulthood, in which he tripped and fell off the "planned road for male achievement." Instinctively, he knew that if he was to come to full maturity, he

1 Nouwen, *Spiritual Direction*, 99.

would need to face his reality, pick himself up, dust himself off, and get back on the path. While marching forward with his head held high, from time-to-time Brad could reach back and touch the memory of this misstep. He had stored it deep within a dark corner of his backpack.

There is not a lot of writing about how men seek and find God. More is written about how men succeed and search for meaning through the rewards of upward mobility—success, productivity, achievement, the acquisition of resources—and pride in their progeny. Most men, actually most human beings, do not stop to name and explore their flaws, limitations, and weaknesses—wondering if there is anything that can be learned from the dark side of life.

Brad's search for God has not come through success—more through embracing the meaning of the six words: "God writes straight with crooked lines." His path, one that he might not have chosen, has been one of finding God in adversity. When Brad and his wife, Janice, had been married for ten years and had two children, their four-year-old son, Erik, suffered severe seizures on a plane flight. While Janice, a competent and experienced nurse, could identify and quell the immediate trauma, neither she nor Erik's doctors could repair their son's damaged brain. While Erik grew physically into adulthood, his mental development leveled at the age of a four-year-old. Marriage, family, and Brad's role as father/protector took a sharp left turn. Where to go from there?

In his own mental and emotional distress, Brad sought solace and balance through psychological counseling. It was through this counselor that Brad was referred to "a spiritual director." He found one in a Catholic nun, Sister Jeanne Fallon, CSJ, who introduced him to the spiritual exercises of Saint Ignatius of Loyola, a disciplined and focused mode of daily prayer. She walked with him as he steadied his feet in his faith during this turbulent time.

Sometime later, Brad was fortunate to meet Gordon Moreland, SJ, a Jesuit priest, who became both his friend and spiritual guide for the next twenty-seven years. Acting on key principles of Ignatian spirituality, Brad came to realize that God wasn't found only in church and in times of prayer, but that God could be found everywhere, in everyone and in each human interaction—even those that he found most challenging. God could be found within his own very human heart and sometimes restless soul.

Like Jesus, who from time to time went to a deserted place to find peace and to pray, for several decades Brad has discovered the hiddenness and wonder of the California desert as a place to center himself, to breathe more deeply and to hand his life over to God again . . . and again.

He shares a few of his solitary desert ventures with his readers, taking us to hidden, quiet places where he eagerly stretched the perimeters of his manly soul.

Henri Nouwen, who wrote a good deal, sometimes wrestling with his words and message, noted that "one of the most satisfying aspects of writing is that it can open in us deep wells of hidden treasures that are beautiful for us as well as for others to see."[2]

Thank you, Brad, for inviting us to your desert place and showing us the depth of your life experience through the hidden treasure of your well.

Eileen McNerney, CSJ

2 Nouwen, *Bread for the Journey*, 90.

Acknowledgments

THANK YOU TO THOSE who read the manuscript and offered important criticism, ideas, and reviews: Dr. Walter Brueggemann of Columbia Theological Seminary; Dr. Ronald Dart, University of Fraser Valley, British Columbia; Dr. David Jasper of the University of Glasgow, Scotland; Father Ron Rolheiser, OMI; Sister Benedicta Ward SLG, Oxford University, England; Dr. Belden Lane, Saint Louis University; Larry Budner, MD, Santa Ana, California; Luan Mendel, Mammoth Lakes, California; Toni Mendoza, Tustin, California; Dr. Jack Miles, University of California at Irvine; Steve Lopardo, Esq., Fallbrook, California; Chris Langley, Lone Pine, California; Michael Prather, Alabama Hills, California; Monsignor John Urell, Laguna Niguel, California; Pastor Georg Nüglisch, Magdeburg, Germany; Dr. Francis X. Clooney, SJ, Harvard Divinity School; Dr. Sheryl Kajawa-Holbrook, Claremont School of Theology; Tom Hamilton, Jr. Hermosa Beach, California.

Thank you to Sister Eileen McNerney CSJ, for writing the foreword to this book. Sister Eileen and I have worked on several projects in Santa Ana over the past thirty years. In 1999 we were founders of Hands Together—A Center for Children, offering three early childhood education centers offering preliteracy programs, and offering preschool education for working-poor families and homeless mothers and children.

Thank you to my spiritual directors, Father Gordon Moreland SJ and Father Domenico de Raimondo MSPS, whose prayerful encouragements have guided me through many interior deserts over the past thirty years.

Finally, thank you to Denis Clarke and Source Books. Denis is the copy-editor of this book and lovingly polished the rough work. I tell my friends that as a British publisher and editor, he translates my work into

English. Over the years, we have shared a ministry with the poor and homeless in Orange County and I am blessed to have his partnership in this project.

Chapter One

Into the Desert

The soul feeds on what takes us to the edge.
But we don't go there willingly.

—BELDEN LANE[1]

WHAT FOLLOWS IS THE story of my seeking God and how the desert became the place for grace-filled encounters with the Lord.

A spiritual oasis blooms within several acres of green lawns, rose bushes, desert plants, and winding walkways between Saint Joseph Hospital and a complex of convent residences for the Sisters of Saint Joseph of Orange in California. A path leads past a park bench where a nun gazes at rose bushes, toward a Spanish-style building which is the Center for Spiritual Development. The Sisters of Saint Joseph of Orange founded the Center decades ago to train spiritual directors and to provide spiritual direction for retreatants. As the program grew, weekend workshops and summer seminars hosted some of the best-known retreat leaders and writers on spirituality. Participants and topics linked the world religions and the diverse denominations of Christianity. But the Sisters had run into a problem: few men attended programs at the Center.

One Saturday morning, I am in a conference room at the Center for Spiritual Development with twenty other men: priests, pastors, deacons,

---

1. Lane, *Great Conversation*, 4.

and laity from the Roman Catholic Church and several Protestant churches. We have been invited to be a "think tank" of topics and workshops that
could appeal to men. All participants have had experience in church men's
groups.

Center Director Cindy Mueller facilitates a fast-paced, intense brain-
storming with our group on spiritual issues for men and possible workshop
programs. One participant stands out for me: Father Jim Clarke, Director
of New Evangelization for the Roman Catholic Diocese of Los Angeles. He
speaks with gentle authority, honed from many years of facilitating workshops for men.

Father Clarke shares, "Men's ways are different We tend to block experiences that would touch us. We change only if we must: when life falls
apart. We don't do our 'shadow work' to puncture our egos (the false self
that we present to people). At the core of men's spirituality is transformation of our pain. Rituals and contemplative prayer are ways that lead us
forward to surrender to God's great love for us."

Father Clarke's colleague, Franciscan priest and founder of the Center
for Action and Contemplation in New Mexico, Richard Rohr, OFM, devel-
ops the concepts of false self and true self for us:

> . . . there is a necessary suffering that cannot be avoided, which
> Jesus calls "losing our very life," or losing what I and others call
> the "false self." Your false self is your role, title, and personal image
> that is largely a creation of your own mind and attachments. It will
> and must die in exact correlation to how much you want the Real.
> . . Your True Self is who you objectively are from the beginning,
> in the mind and heart of God. . . It is your substantial self, your
> absolute identity. . . The surrendering of our false self, which we
> have usually taken for our absolute identity, yet is merely a rela-
> tive identity, is the necessary suffering needed to find "the pearl
> of great price" that is always hidden inside this lovely but passing
> shell.[2]

These insights help me to remember with gratitude how my own false
self was punctured when life fell apart, and how I eventually fell into God's
arms, experiencing God's amazing grace.

I am no model for male spirituality. During my first twenty years as
a parish priest, I hope I communicated the gospel of Jesus, but that gospel
was more from my head than from my heart.

2. Rohr, *Falling Upward*, 85–86.

This was not my first time at the Center for Spiritual Development. Now, sitting around that table with other men who have been seeking God in their lives was a powerful homecoming. It was here, in 1990, that I first sought spiritual direction with Sister Jeanne Fallon, CSJ, and began the year-long curriculum of the Spiritual Exercises of Saint Ignatius Loyola.

Three years earlier, our family had been turned upside down.

Father's Day, 1987. My wife, Janice, ten-year old daughter Katie, and four-year old son Erik were on an American Airline flight from Los Angeles to Logan Airport, Boston, Massachusetts.

We were on our way to our annual vacation in a small New England town for a month with Janice's parents. Now I could begin to let go of that caffeine-and-adrenaline-driven life of intense multitasking and enjoy this time with family.

Half-way to Boston, our son began to convulse violently. My wife, who is an RN, recognized an intense seizure immediately. We could see that Erik would relax for a few seconds and then continue shaking violently. Status epilepticus: a life-threatening condition of constant convulsions. After an hour of this agony, the airplane was given priority landing at Logan Airport. Paramedics rushed Erik off to Massachusetts General Hospital. For the entire month of that "vacation", we were back and forth to the hospital and Erik went in and out of coma and several near-death events. Erik had encephalitis, inflammation of the brain, the cause at that point was unknown. When we left the hospital, he could not walk or talk and did not recognize us.

Suddenly, my carefully organized life with my Franklin Planner, numbered priorities for each day, jam-packed schedules of meetings and events—these were no longer what drove me. Like an earthquake had hit, we had to drop it all, and focus on care for Erik.

For the next dozen years, we were in and out of Orange County hospitals, trying to tame the tiger of these horrible seizures. We could be at the dinner table, everything seeming okay, then Erik might cough, which could mean two weeks of nausea and not eating, until we went back to the hospital again. It would seem like his body would break in the sudden seizures, and when they would not stop, we would call the paramedics once again to take him to the Emergency Room. All those years we searched for the right medications to calm the seizure storm.

I went to psychiatrist Dr. Bob Phillips for help with the depression that was pulling me down, the deep grief and ache for the suffering of our son.

Early on, I remember him saying, "You know, Brad, I can see you are trying to manage and control your life and the life of your wife and family, with no room for God to intervene. When you wake up, and let go of this frantic need to control, maybe God can help you."

Dr. Bob recommended spiritual direction as additional help for me. He sent me across the street from his office in Orange, California, to Sister Jeanne Fallon, CSJ, and I began the Spiritual Exercises, developed by the Spanish mystic Ignatius Loyola five hundred years ago. For about forty-five minutes each day for twelve months I practiced contemplative meditation on a scripture passage, moving through the key events in the life of Jesus. Sister Jeanne encouraged me to use my imagination and to enter the various Biblical scenes as if I were there, asking God to reveal to me what the passage meant to me. I noticed a shift in how I approached scripture after this. In seminary, I was trained to bring an analytical mind to the passages. Now I hear the scriptures as if they were written for me to hear and read.

I would follow that part of the meditation with something mundane like mowing the lawn, washing dishes, doing laundry. An hour later I would write in a journal what I was thinking and feeling and what I thought God's hopes and desires were for me at that time. I met with Sister Jeanne once a week to review what was happening within me.

As a spiritual director, Sister Jeanne helped me to deepen my relationship with God. She shared stories about her own encounters with God. Sister Jeanne had recently returned from a ten-year mission in Papua New Guinea.

In 1994, Father Gordon Moreland, SJ, became my spiritual director. He told me about his teenage years working the family vineyard in eastern Washington State. He used a simile: new vine plantings were like dried twigs. His job was to identify the right buds and then train their shoots to create two strong lower branches and two strong top branches. He had to develop an intuition about which new buds needed to be nurtured. In his ministry as spiritual director, he prayed to have the discernment and intuition to guide the sprouting energies of a seeker toward God's desires for that person.

I remember Sister Jeanne saying, "You know, Brad, this will not be a program of spiritual sedation for you. Hidden parts of your life will come into the light where you will have difficult work with the Lord."

For many years I had traveled the Mojave Desert, hunting out old mining camps and Native American sites. Advent was coming up in November, a good time to visit the desert. Sister Jeanne suggested that perhaps I could go off for a retreat in the desert. I calendared four weekdays, received permission from the parish and Janice and contemplated this opportunity to draw closer to the Lord.

Because I used to visit the Owens Valley of the Eastern Sierra, California, which is in the shadow of Mount Whitney, I began reading on the area. My mental self needed an isolated site with a story, a history. My reading led me to an obscure site off Highway 395 south of Lone Pine: Rose Springs.

I headed out early in the morning up Highway 395, past volcanic cliffs and parallel to the snow-capped Sierra Nevada mountains. A narrow paved road leading to a power plant took me to a hidden notch-canyon. I stepped out into the cold November morning, walking down into clumps of prickly sagebrush toward a square stone structure. I can still remember how the moist morning dew released the sweet scent of the great basin sage. A verdant outcrop loomed over the structure, which must be the seep of Rose Springs. Fifty yards away, hidden in sage brush, were two long concrete basins, which might be water troughs for horses. A pile of broken bricks lay at the base of the cistern. This must have been the stagecoach station for the Mojave and Keeler Stage Line, which had burned in 1868 in a Paiute attack. All this visible history is only one mile off busy Highway 395!

The sheltered quiet in this hidden canyon invited me to settle down and stay awhile.

A basalt cliff soared to my right and I could see there was a large cave in it. I carefully climbed rocky debris to the entrance of the cave. I heard the frantic flutter of wings, as a huge white owl flew out of the cave, shrieking. I entered the cave, and finding a large flat rock, sat down to look out on the vast desert landscape. I could not see or hear any sign of cars traveling on the highway. What a delightful spot for contemplation!

After a few minutes, the intense concentration and fatigue from the four-hour drive dissipated. I remember the anxiety and fear I carried at that time centered in my gut, an almost constant feeling of dread during Erik's recent hospitalization.

God sparked a memory from the scriptures: The prophet Elijah entered a cave just like this as he fled Queen Jezebel's posse of soldiers. In the protective enclosure of a desert cave on Mount Horeb, panic and depression pressed upon his soul. After an anxious dark night in the cave, upon awakening Elijah hears the soft voice of God: "What are you doing here?" "Nothing at all," is the reply.[3]

Elijah was learning that *being* in God rather than *doing* for God can be the ultimate sign of faithfulness.

This memory from scripture is a reminder about the spiritual challenge—for men in particular. We can look at the invitation to seek a deeper life with God as a work project and a task. We can be hard on ourselves about not praying in the right way and not following someone's lists of spiritual disciplines. We read books about prayer and spirituality (or, like me, we write them). But finally, when we are exhausted and at the end of our rope, we can stop doing and we can be, we can rest in the Lord. I can rest in the Lord on this rock, in this cave, in this canyon surrounded by desert wilderness.

The journey to Rose Springs was a foundational desert experience for me. It gave me God's close presence in a wild place. The chronic dread inside me lifted to be replaced by consoling feelings of hope, God's gifts, and joy at having found this quiet canyon set apart.

I had only a vague memory of the desert fathers and mothers from seminary classes. But over the next thirty years, I discovered a whole genre of writing on the spirituality of the desert. As I read the works of Belden Lane, Thomas Merton, Richard Rohr, Ron Rolheiser, and indigenous writers such as Leslie Marmon Silko, I was reminded that the desert milieu was the spiritual crucible for the Hebrew people's encounter with God at Sinai and their forty-year wandering, which gave them a complete dependency on God's grace. The desert was where Jesus found his destiny as the Messiah. It was where fourth-century Christian men and women, rejecting the comfortable faith of Christianity as the imperial Roman-approved religion, retreated to the deserts of Egypt, Syria, and Palestine, to seek silence, solitude, and a raw, purer life with God. A desert cave is where Mohammed experienced the call to prophesy.

And so I discovered "desert spirituality" as a way of seeking God in a wilderness testing-ground through silence, prayer, and solitude.

---

3. 1 Kings 19:9–18.

Father Brad Karelius, Owens Lake Trail, California 2015. Photo by Janice Karelius.

Belden C. Lane, Professor Emeritus of Spirituality at Saint Louis University, describes the invitation of the desert to men who seek God:

> This is what the desert does best, taking us to the end of ourselves, physically, culturally, spiritually. It alternately tricks and teases us into reaching for what lies beyond, for what's entirely too much for us to handle. Losing control is the point. You'll only be satisfied, the desert says, by what you give up trying to comprehend.[4]

Over the three or four days of that first desert retreat, walking in silence and solitude in the desert landscape, I could see and hear what had been speaking to me all along: a soft voice of loving kindness and enfolding love.

Desert spirituality has evolved from personal encounters in the desert to graduate courses on spirituality. At the Oblate School of Theology in San Antonia Texas, Dr. Douglas Christie offered this course description:

4. Lane, *Great Conversation*, 137.

What does it mean to enter the desert? To dwell there, either by choice or necessity? To engage with and respond to its beauty, its emptiness and desolation? To discover there unexpected inner resources, the potential for life-altering transformation, renewed capacity for life in community? As a metaphor for the deep un-knowability of God, for the stillness, silence, and emptiness in which a meeting with the divine becomes possible, the image of the desert has become one of the central images of the spiritual life in the Christian tradition.[5]

I wrote this book with three goals in mind.

First, to help you and other men admit your deep longing for God. The false self (this is who I am, this is what I have, this is what I have accomplished, this is what people think of me) dominates our identity, propelling our restless passions and desires. Peace, love, hope and joy will be found as we awaken to our true self, our Christ-self, that rests in God. As Saint Augustine says, "You have made us for yourself, Lord and our hearts are restless until they rest in you."[6] I believe our deepest desire is communion and friendship with our Lord Jesus Christ.

Second. to encourage you to make a journey into the wilderness or desert, to seek silence and solitude as a gateway to contemplative encounters with God. I will offer specific guidance for preparation for a desert retreat.

Third, to encourage you to seek the support of other men in your spiritual journey, including men who are not Christian or members of a Christian congregation. A parish men's spirituality group and spiritual direction will remind you that we need each other in our journey with God.

As I share my spiritual journey as a man, I will reflect on the various roles we may have: father, friend to other men, husband, priest, teacher. I will share stories about men of God in my life. And I will offer forms of prayer that are especially suited for men.

---

5. "Desert Spirituality," *Oblate School of Theology,* https://ost.edu/ma-spirituality/desert-spirituality/.

6 Augustine, *Confessions,* 3.

Chapter Two

The Singing Sand Dunes
of Death Valley

The feeling of it may at times come sweeping like a gentle tide pervading the mind with a tranquil mood of deepest worship. It may pass over into a more set and lasting attitude of the soul, continuing, as it were, thrillingly vibrant and resonant, until at last it dies away and the soul resumes its 'profane,' non-religious mood of everyday experience. [. . .] It has its crude, barbaric antecedents and early manifestations, and again it may be developed into something beautiful and pure and glorious. It may become the hushed, trembling, and speechless humility of the creature in the presence of—whom or what? In the presence of that which is a Mystery inexpressible and above all creatures.

—RUDOLF OTTO[1]

WHAT IS THE MEANING of the enticing allure I feel in my gut? I gaze at an expanse of rippled, curving sand dunes, hundred-foot mountains of quartz and granite granules, changing from pink to purple in the late afternoon sunlight. Awe and wonder at the vastness invite me to enter and wander; desert wildness warns of danger.

1. Otto, *Idea of the Holy*, 12.

9

I stand at the edge of the parking lot for the Mesquite Flat Sand Dunes, off Highway 190, the main road through Death Valley National Park, about a mile east of Stovepipe Wells.

For the past two hours I have driven eighty miles from my base in Lone Pine, over two mountain ranges, with hairpin turns, watching for reckless motorcyclists, who have been known to drive off the road to their death. Fighter pilots from China Lake fly low, buzzing the highway. Their afterburners shake my car. It took intense concentration to make it here safely as I wait for my soul to catch up with my body. Busy, numbed mind. Dry mouth. Fatigue.

At 4 PM, at the Mesquite Flat parking lot, most tourists are leaving. No wind, clear skies, 75°F on a spring day in March, two hours before the sun sets behind the Sierra Nevada. I cannot resist any longer and I walk toward the highest dune.

The ground is hard playa, which retains the pools of winter rain until the sun evaporates the water and the dried mud becomes a mosaic of cracked clay, reminding me that the floor of the dunes is an ancient lakebed. The loose, deep sand comes quickly as I climb into the dunes.

Here and there are spots of green: creosote and mesquite. Their dried pods were a life staple for the Timbisha Shoshone people. Water has seeped deep into the sand, creating occasional pockets of life. Small burrows emanate from the sides of the brush, home to kit fox, scorpions, snakes, and jackrabbits. When summer sun heats the dunes in the morning, a lounge of lizards darts about, including the whitish-gray foot-long desert iguana.

I follow a well-traveled trail to the highest dune from the top of which I see a vast sea of undulating sand. I gingerly walk the rim of the high dune to the left for a hundred yards and notice that there has been no recent foot traffic up here.

I must take my mind off the highway and become sharply aware right now of what is in front of me: the steep edge of a dune. It is like walking on a tightrope. My body wants to lean, which would mean tumbling down the sandy slope. Focus on this step, now the next one. Let go of that last step and concentrate on this one. When I look around at the expansive mountains of sand, I suddenly find myself slipping and sliding down the dune, falling to my knees, losing control, and tumbling down. I dig in with my hiking boots and try to climb back up the steep slope.

Dr. Bobbi Patterson, Religion Professor at Emory University has given an interesting presentation about burnout and resilience She remembers her difficult experience walking a dune in the Sinai Desert in Egypt:

> Pause and Regroup, notice where you are and what's happening. That reset of my awareness helped me discern the angles of approach I needed to slowly make my way back to the group at the top. But each step brought its own tipsiness. . . Like riding a riptide. I learned to go with the line of fall on the dune rather than fight it.[2]

As I concentrate on my awareness of each step, I regain the crest of the dune. Moving westward for several hundred yards, I cautiously descend into a deep hollow, a high circle of dunes surround me. The intense exertion has purged my busy mind.

I breathe and become as quiet as the silence. No wind. My wobbly, fatigued legs pull me down upon the soft sand. No Mind.

Awe, huge emptiness, silence. The Presence seems close to me. As this circle of sand surrounds me, God's love enfolds me. The busy mind, following map directions, listening to music on the car radio, thoughts about yesterday and tomorrow, that busy mind now rests. Awe, emptiness, and silence.

Empty desert landscape like this heightens my senses. The Now becomes paramount. I remember what pulls me out into these desert spaces. For many years, during my son Erik's health crises, retreats like this were a respite from the intense daily routine of his care. Now that his health has stabilized to some extent, the feelings of anxiety and fear about his future have changed to gratitude for how God has been with us all along.

Visitors to desert spaces like this have various perspectives as they walk and contemplate. Sitting here on cool sand, a warm winter day, protected from wind by the encircling dunes, the foggy veil of consciousness lifts. The gracious, loving Presence is beside me. As I write these words, many months after this experience, this foundational remembering enlivens my sense of God's care and love.

I lose sense of time, but time has passed as the sun is now just above the Sierra Nevada and darkness is less than an hour away.

A thought arises: a memory from the world religions class I taught for forty-five years at Saddleback Community College: the haunting insight from German philosopher Rudolf Otto. Otto was a theologian and

---

2. Patterson, *Building Resilience through Contemplative Practice*, 52.

philosopher of comparative religions. His classic book, *The Idea of the Holy*, contemplates the numinous, the deeply-sensed encounter with the holy that is beyond words, "A non-rational, non-sensory experience or feeling whose primary and immediate object is outside the self."[3]

Christian writer C. S. Lewis reflects on the numinous in his *The Problem of Pain*:

> You would feel wonder and a certain shrinking—a sense of inadequacy to cope with such a visitant and of prostration before it (the Holy)—an emotion which might be expressed in Shakespeare's words 'Under it my genius is rebuked.' This feeling may be described as awe, and the object which excites it as the Numinous.[4]

Extraordinary encounters with awe and wonder can evoke a sense of a merciful Presence. We do not conjure this, it just happens. We are drawn toward the Presence by an innate holy longing and at the same time we are aware that this Presence has great power. In our awareness, we come forward in awe, and step back in fear and dread. Otto's classic insight describes the ineffable encounter with the sacred.

Landscape like this endless sand invites awe and wonder. But sand dunes are also deadly, as recent events remind me.

Visitor attendance in Death Valley peaks in the summer, the most brutal season, when temperatures range from 115°F to 125°F. Recently, on an early June afternoon, a tour bus stopped at the Mesquite Flat Sand Dunes for the passengers to step out and take photos. The dry heat would have taken their breath away as they left the air-conditioned bus. The driver warned the tourists that they must return to the bus within ten minutes. A Frenchman, Guy Brossart, must have become captivated by the allure of the sand dunes. The bus driver waited for an hour, then called the Death Valley Park rangers, who began the search. Brossart's body was found just four hundred yards from the parking lot. He had succumbed to heat exhaustion.[5]

In August, the month in which Death Valley often breaks world heat-index records, a Japanese tourist exited the bus and walked into the dunes to take photographs. You only have a few minutes in this intense heat before the sun fries your body, sucking out every bit of moisture, leaving you fatigued, disoriented and unable to walk. The hypnotic draw of the dunes has power to pull you further and further in—"Just a few more steps and I

3. Alles, *Autobiographical and Social Essays*, 30.

4. Lewis, *Problem of Pain*, 5–6.

5. *Mammoth Times*, June 9, 2014.

will turn around." But the brain stops working as the sun beats down upon you. The body of the Japanese tourist was found at sunset a mile from the parking lot.

John Van Dyke, the grandfather of American desert writers, describes sand dunes in his 1901 classic *The Desert*:

> The shifting sands! Slowly they move, wave upon wave, drift upon drift; but by day and by night they gather, gather, gather. They over-whelm, they bury, they destroy, and then a spirit of restlessness seizes them, and they move off elsewhere, swirl upon swirl, line upon line, in serpentine windings that enfold some new growth or fill in some new valley in the waste. So, it happens that the surface of the desert is far from being a permanent affair.[6]

Of the five sand dunes within Death Valley National Park, the Mesquite Flat Sand Dunes are the easiest to visit. The Cottonwood Mountains to the north are the likely source for the grains of quartz and feldspar that have created these dunes.

The dramatic fluctuation between freezing winter snow and melting summer heat wears down the rocky heights of the mountains. Monsoonal summer storms beat upon the barren slopes of the mountains. There are violent flash floods, breaking loose the rocks, grinding them into sand, dumping the debris into alluvial fans which spread out from the narrow canyons onto the valley floor.

It does not take much of a breeze to move the sand particles. But the wind is often violent, creating blinding sandstorms. A Department of the Interior guide describes the formation of the sand dunes in Death Valley:

> Once sand begins to pile up, ripples and dunes can form. Wind continues to move sand up to the top of the pile until the pile is so steep that it collapses under its own weight. The collapsing sand comes to rest when it reaches just the right steepness to keep the dune stable. This angle, usually about 30–34 degrees, is called the angle of repose. Every pile of loose particles has a unique angle of repose, depending upon the properties of the material it's made of.
>
> The repeating cycle of sand inching up the windward side to the dune crest, then slipping down the dune's slip face allows the dune to inch forward migrating in the direction the wind blows. As you might guess, all of this climbing then slipping leaves its mark on the internal structure of the dune.[7]

6. Van Dyke, *Desert*, 28.

7. U. S. Department of the Interior, U. S. Geological Survey.

Sand avalanches moved by compressed air can cause the sand to sing! Yes, the sand dune can produce singing or booming sounds. YouTube presents an excellent video of the singing sand dunes.[8]

Conditions must be exactly right: sand grains 0.1 to 0.5mm in diameter, silica within the sand, and the right humidity and heat. Researchers have found that the best chance for hearing singing sand dunes in Death Valley is with intense heat, the most dangerous time to walk in the dunes. The sound can be started by wind or a person walking on the crest of a high dune. While the dunes of Mesquite Flat do not sing because of the water that is present, the Eureka Dunes, at the far eastern end of the park can sing.

Science writer Dennis Chang reports in the New York Times:

> Since at least the time of Marco Polo, desert travelers have heard the songs of the dunes, a loud—up to 115 decibels—deep hum that can last several minutes.
>
> Scientists already knew that avalanches generated the sounds but were not sure how. One thought had been that the force of an avalanche could cause an entire dune to resonate like a flute or a violin. But if that were true, dunes of different sizes and shapes should produce a cacophony of notes instead of one characteristic tone.[9]

The Timbisha Shoshone people have lived in Death Valley for a thousand years. I cannot imagine how a people could survive here, but they worked intently as hunters and gatherers, moving to the cooler, higher elevations in the summer heat. The mild winters gave time to store up pine nuts and mesquite beans, their main staples. Mule deer, bighorn sheep, jackrabbits and chuckwalla lizards provided meat. Death Valley to them was a land of abundance until outsiders invaded during the 1849 Gold Rush and they discovered borax in these hills. This changed everything. The original people were displaced, and their survival has been a struggle. It was not until 2000, when President Clinton signed the Timbisha Shoshone Homeland Act, that seventy-five hundred acres would be returned to the tribe.

Through my writings on desert spirituality, my life has been enriched by connections with scholars and others who have found meaning in desert

---

8. Singing Sand Dunes, *National Geographic*, https://www.youtube.com/watch?v=4mbypyJjqhk.

9. Chang, *New York Times*, Secrets of the singing Sand Dunes, July 25, 2006.https://www.nytimes.com/2006/07/25/science/25find.html.

explorations. I have a new friend in Fred Mercadante, campus minister at the University of Scranton, a Jesuit University in Pennsylvania.

I recently discovered that for several years Fred has led desert retreat experiences for students in Death Valley during December. Inspired by the school's Jesuit foundation, the students spend five days in contemplation while they explore different desert landscapes, including the Eureka Sand Dunes.

In the Christian tradition of desert spirituality, the desert is a place of discernment and prayer. Fred offers this retreat experience to help the students be intentional about their faith journey and to "go to deeper places, perhaps even places that feel uncomfortable at first."

This desert retreat guides students to pray in Nature, build community with each other, and fosters personal growth. As Jesus experienced his deepening connection with the Father in his forty days in the desert, these students come closer to their true selves, their Christ-selves.

One participant, Bryan Gorczyca, shared: "The week spent in Death Valley tested every member of our group physically, mentally and spiritually through many tasks and challenges which brought us all to a new outlook on ourselves, others and Mother Nature. At no time in my life have I experienced such peace with the world as I did in the silence of reflection on this retreat... I have come out a better version of myself."[10]

Zane Grey always personally experienced the landscapes described in his memorable western novels. From *Stars of Sand,* Grey writes:

> The sand dunes again! Clear, soft, blown clean by the wind, rippled as by shore waves, rising from the desert in long smooth rounded slopes, climbing and swelling and mounting, curved, scalloped, knife-edged, lacy, exquisitely silver, on and up, alluring steps toward the infinite blue![11]

There are five places in Death Valley National Park where you can find sand dunes.

You can access Mesquite Flat Dunes from the parking lot off Highway 190, near Stovepipe Wells. Covering a vast area, the highest dune is about one-hundred feet.

Eureka Dunes is more difficult to get to, from Big Pine, off Highway 395, via twenty-eight miles of paved road and twenty-one miles of graded

---

10. *National Catholic Reporter*, March 22, 2018.
11. Grey, *Stairs of Sand: A Western Story,* loc. 2728.

dirt. Most autos can travel this road, but make sure you avoid stormy weather. Possibly the tallest dunes in North America, their isolation led to the development of plants and animals found nowhere else in the world, such as the Devil's Hole pupfish, the Panamint kangaroo rat, golden carpet, Death Valley monkeyflower, and the Eureka Dunes evening primrose.

Saline Valley Dunes have infrequent visitors as the area is remote. The dunes cover a large area. Come prepared for difficult desert driving and dynamic weather changes.

Panamint Dunes are off Highway 190, five miles down an unmarked dirt road, followed by a three-mile hike. Because of the slope of the dunes, there are dramatic views of the valley.

Ibex Springs is near Saratoga Springs but hidden behind desert hills. Expect a one-mile hike. You may encounter the Mojave fringe-toed lizard as you hike in the dunes there.

The best time to visit the dunes is between November and April. Avoid the summer months and any other hot days. Carry two liters of water per person for short hikes; four liters for longer.

Chapter Three

Owens Lake Project
From Desolation to Consolation

Great numbers of water birds are in sight along the lake shore—
avocets, phalaropes, ducks. Large flocks of shorebirds in flight over
the water in the distance, wheeling about in mass, now silvery now
dark, against the gray blue of the water. There must be literally thousands of birds within sight of this one spot.

—Joseph Grinnell[1]

THE SILVER FREIGHTLINER EIGHTEEN–WHEEL truck lies on its side in the
southbound lane of Highway 395 in Olancha, California, four hours north
of Los Angeles. My Oldsmobile Bravada, a heavyweight car, shakes in the
hard wind, as I wait in a line of cars in the northbound lane. The road is
littered with hundreds of plastic water bottles bearing the logo which is on
the side of the truck: Crystal Geyser Water. The bottling factory is a mile
north. The beverage holder at my car console holds a half-opened bottle of
Crystal Geyser. Through the cottonwood trees to my left, I can see Olancha
Peak of the Sierra Nevada Mountains, which appears on the water bottle

1. Grinnell, quoted in "Birds are Rediscovering Owens Lake," *Los Angeles Times,*
January 21, 2002.

label. The truck driver sits on the ground, supported by a bystander holding a compress to the man's bleeding head.

I recognize the Highway Patrol officer, Paul Pino, as he approaches my car. He lives in Lone Pine, thirty minutes north. Holding a wind monitor above his head he grimaces and exclaims, "Horrible! Seventy miles-an-hour gusts. There are two more big-rigs blown over up the road. We have to close the highway until it is safe."

Behind me, a detour road leads to Death Valley and around Owens Lake. The officer directs traffic as we make U-turns. The wind gusts continue to ruthlessly shake my car.

I see the Ranch House Café and decide to wait out the windstorm over there as I eat lunch. In a corner window I watch the wind bend and shake century-old cottonwoods. A sudden crack followed by a thud. A huge tree branch falls to the ground in front of me, shattering some wild rose bushes.

In the distance, a white tornado cloud of chemical dust whirls thousands of feet above Owens Lake. The wind blows eastward toward the lakeside village of Keeler. Noxious alkali storms like this can carry four million tons of dust at a time containing carcinogens such as cadmium, nickel and arsenic. This is the most polluted air in the United States.

It would not be difficult for these hundreds of drivers heading north to look briefly eastward at that poisonous cloud of dust and the dry lake and think: "That must be the septic basin of the Owens Valley. Who cares? I sure wouldn't want to live around here."

This dying lake has a grand history. The lake basin itself may be one million years old. Twelve thousand years ago, it contained two hundred square miles of water two hundred feet deep. Water from melting glaciers of the waning Ice Age overflowed the lake southward into Rose Valley and China Lake. You can visit the ancient shores of the lake.

A litle over a hundred years ago, the lake still covered one hundred and eight square miles, to a depth of between twenty-five and fifty feet. The water began to disappear when the Los Angeles Aqueduct opened in 1913, diverting Owens River water away from the lake.The once vibrant ecosystem that sustained millions of birds and animals and plants—not to mention the ranches, farms, orchards, and mines—dried into an alkali-encrusted sump.

Two-hours pass. Cars move slowly forward. I join the snaking throng of traffic heading north. In thirty minutes, I am in Lone Pine, standing on the balcony outside room fifty at the Dow Villa Motel. The hovering cloud of nasty dust expands, spreading out toward Lone Pine and the Sierra Nevada.

I have been making my Advent and Lenten retreats to the Owens Valley since 1980, staying in Lone Pine and making many friends, among whom two remarkable public-school teachers, Michael Prather, and Chris Langley. Knowing them has revealed a great secret about the Owens Valley. They could have been teaching at a top Eastern prep school. But they chose Lone Pine. Michael and Chris developed community organizing skills, bringing residents together to create notable public projects: The Lone Pine Film History Museum, the Alabama Hills National Scenic Area and the Owens Lake Bird Festival.

I believe that living in this history-soaked, spirit-laden land, experiencing the sacredness of this haunting, achingly beautiful valley, must inspire and empower the people to be assertive in protecting and renewing forlorn sites such as Owens Lake.

I found out that there are many other people who are equally passionate about the ecological vitality of the Owens Valley and skilled at building a powerful coalition between local non-profit organizations. That coalition along with Inyo County government forced the City of Los Angeles and the Los Angeles Department of Water and Power (LADWP) into the courtroom. The battle between these "small-town folks" and the big city seemed hopeless. Eventually the courts forced LADWP to take responsibility for the damage to the lake and putting lives at risk, as for a century Los Angeles had drained off the aqueous life-blood of this desert land.

Los Angeles Times writer Louis Sagahun has reported on Owens Valley for decades, focusing on the hand-to-hand courtroom battles between Los Angeles and Inyo County. He joyfully reported on what was to become the successful renovation of the Lake.

> In what is now hailed as an astonishing environmental success, Nature quickly responded. First to appear were brine flies. Then came masses of waterfowl and shorebirds that feed on the insects.[2]

Here is a spiritual exercise that I call "A Mindful Walk through an Alkali Marsh."

Again, the best months for a lake visit are between November and April, avoiding windy days. And I can't say this enough: be sure you have ample drinking water.

---

2. Sagahun, "Owens Lake," *Los Angeles Times*, April 28, 2018.

Directions: driving north on Highway 395, a few miles south of Lone Pine, turn right on to Highway 136. Note the sign to Death Valley. Immediately turn right into the parking lot for the Lone Pine Interagency Visitor Center. This is the best place to find information about the Owens Valley and Death Valley. An excellent bookstore features books about the area and many free brochures. Look for *The Owens Lake Trails*. This will guide you to various access points within Owens Lake. Pages 6–7 have directions to the Plaza Route.

When you leave the Visitor Center, turn right and continue for 10.2 miles on Highway 136. You will pass the remains of the silver ore smelting village of Swansea. Following the map, turn onto the Plaza T30–1 access route. Continue the route down the hill for half a mile toward the eastern shore of Owens Lake. Turn left where the road faces the managed vegetation wetlands. You will see scattered plants and trees bringing life to the once barren playa. Continue down the road, turning right to access the Plaza Trailhead parking area, which is on both sides of the road. Watch out for heavy equipment vehicles that frequently travel this road to continue the maintenance and renovation of the lake.

Begin to walk the gravel pathway leading to the Plover Wing Plaza, one-half mile to the north.

Instead of a spirited trek to that destination, I invite you to make a walking meditation. This is an exercise to increase "mindfulness." While this term is prevalent in New Age spirituality, the practice of mindfulness is twenty-five hundred years old, going back to the original teachings of Siddhartha Gautama, the Buddha, the Awakened One.

Buddha was a spiritual doctor who diagnosed a core problem of human existence: *duhkha* or, dissatisfaction. Life has an impermanent quality, though we continue to cling to people, things, and experiences in a life of illusion. Buddha developed from his own experience the Eight-Fold Path, a lifelong curriculum of guidance to help people find serenity and inner peace. Meditation is the principal method of awakening to the present moment, which the Buddha contends is what is real: the past is a memory that will not come back; the future is always not yet. What we have is the present moment, this present breath, this present heartbeat. Yet, our human tendency is to fixate on the past or the future. Our minds become possessed with anxiety, depression, anger, and frustration. The medicine he prescribes is meditation.

Mindfulness is one way we can bring our attention to the present moment without judgment. While it is not itself prayer, it can be a prelude to prayer.

Let us begin a walking meditation here on the short trail to the Plover Wing Plaza.

I am aware of sensations as I stand on this gravel path. I am aware of the pressure and tension on my feet and legs, my hands hanging down, the weight of my shoulders, back and pelvis. I slowly shift my body weight from left to right and notice how this affects my sense of balance. I shift body weight to my left side, sensing how the right side feels lighter. I shift weight to my right side and allow my awareness to move through muscle to bone, noticing what is hard and soft, tough, and flexible.

Steven V. Smith is a guiding teacher of the Kyaswa Retreat Center in Myanmar. He advises,

> Move slowly as if you are very slowly pouring water from a full vessel into an empty one. Notice all the changes as you shift your weight to the left side. With your eyes open just enough to hold your balance, very slowly peel your right foot off the ground and move it forward and place it back on the ground before you. With your awareness on the right, shift your weight, bring awareness to the left, feel from the hips and buttocks down the sides the whole range of sensations. Continue stepping slowly, keeping your awareness on the sensation.[3]

As you walk with bare awareness, you are not evaluating the experience. You are not looking around, but only a few feet ahead. Thoughts will come and go. If some thought tries to take over, stop and let it pass through. You will probably find resistance within you the first time you try this.

And before you know it, you are at Plover Wing Plaza. In 2016, landscape architect Perry Cardoza was commissioned to create a land art project. At the end of the trail and the mindful walk there is a surprise: a stone and metal shade structure. This land art work is in the shape of the extended wings of the protected snowy plover (which nests at the lake). The sculpture invites restful contemplation. There are Asian landscape influences reflecting Perry Cardoza's time in Japan. Cardoza describes the Plaza:

> The main plaza design was inspired by the nest of the snowy plover. Circular in form this plaza is meant to be the central gathering

---

3. Smith, *Walking Meditation*, https://www.contemplativemind.org/practices/tree/walking-meditation.

space for visitors. The central feature of rock on the plaza that some have named the "Zen Rock" represents a snowy plover, while the other plaza's boulders positioned in large circles around the plaza represent the eggs in the nest.[4]

There are two parts to this remarkable land art: The Plover Wing Plaza and the Owens Valley Trails. You will also notice dune-like constructions that are "whitecaps." Cardoza studied a pre-1912 photograph which showed a deep-water lake and strong winds creating whitecaps. He recreated these whitecaps in his landscape architecture, as noted by the LADWP:

> Looking out over the lake, visitors can see fourteen mound-like structures intended to look like whitecap waves. These metaphorical whitecaps vary in size and are placed in locations that will assist with dust control by keeping surrounding lake particles from being gathered up by the wind. The large rocks used to create the whitecaps [are] habitat for small reptiles, insects and mammals.[5]

I am sitting on a long stone bench in the shade of Plover Wing Plaza. No wind today, only a gentle, warm, salty breeze. I can taste the briny air. A grey-blue mini-lake spreads out before me. Mount Whitney, and the Sierra Nevada are in the distance: a wide-screen, expansive, clear panorama that pulls at my heart and soul. The separation between I, who see, and that which is seen is erased. The water reflects sky, clouds, mountains, birds, and me as I draw closer to the mini-lake.

The medieval mystic Hildegard of Bingen observed, "I have created mirrors in which I consider all the wonders of my originality which will never cease."[6] The Franciscan priest and desert mystic Richard Rohr, OFM, shares that,

> Nature is not a mere scenic backdrop so humans can take over the stage. Creation is in fact a full participant in human transformation, since the outer world absolutely needs to mirror the true inner world. There are not just two sacraments, or even seven; the whole world is a sacrament.[7]

---

4. Langley, "Perry Cardoza's Land Art Project Breaks Ground in the Owens Valley," February 3, 2016, https://www.kcet.org/shows/artbound/perry-cardozas-land-art-project-breaks-ground-in-the-owens-valley.

5. Los Angeles Department of Water and Power, *Owens Lake Trails*, 11.

6. Fox, *Hildegard of Bingen's Book of Divine Works*, 128.

7. Rohr, "Nature as a Mirror of God," March 12, 2018. https://cac.org/nature-as-a-mirror-of-god-2018-03-12/.

Anchored in this place of consolation and contemplation, my human senses, the Creator's gracious gift, pierce the illusion of my controlling observations, awakening deeper intuitive consciousness of holy communion with breathtaking beauty. Spread out before me are carefully-scribed pages of creation's book that joyfully proclaim praise to the Creator. A canticle from the *Book of Common Prayer* gives voice to my meditation:

> Let the earth glorify the Lord,
> praise him and highly exalt him forever.
> Glorify the Lord, O mountains and hills,
> and all that grows upon the earth,
> praise him and highly exalt him forever.
> Glorify the Lord, O springs of water, seas, and streams,
> O whales and all that move in the waters.
> All the birds of the air, glorify the Lord,
> praise him and highly exalt him forever.
> Glorify the Lord, O beasts of the wild,
> and all you flocks and herds.
> O men and women everywhere, glorify the Lord,
> praise him and highly exalt him for ever.[8]

Returning on the trail back to your car, you may continue to explore the lake as you follow a grid of dolomite berms within the lake, which outline several mini-lakes. The remarkable renewal of Owens Lake has resulted in unanticipated wonders. It has created a rich habitat to welcome migrating birds and the elevated berms provide perfect sites for enthusiastic birdwatchers.

Michael Prather is the man who organized early bird counts on Owens Lake. As the bird populations grew, Prather's tenacious efforts rallied strong local support, resulting in an Audubon Society designation of Owens Lake as a Western Hemisphere Shorebird Reserve Network site of international importance.

Affirming a celebrative stance, Marty Adams, Chief Operating Officer of the LADWP said in an interview: "We're extremely proud to be in partnership with Audubon and other groups that worked hand in hand to get to this point. We've created one of the largest projects in the world based on natural solutions for quality-of-life issues."

Let's take the opportunity to practice mindfulness with the birds that have come to the lake. At the outset let me state that I have not been much

---

8. "Song of Creation," *Book of Common Prayer*, 89.

of a birdwatcher—perhaps it has something to do with the fact that for years, my wife Janice has had a large, all-year aviary on the side of our house, where she has raised dozens of parakeets. This winter, she decided to bring her birds into our home where they reside in two large metal cages, "one for the Democrats and one for the Republicans," she advises. People who call us on the phone, hearing the cacophony, think we live in the Amazon jungle.

I found a contemplative friend in David Standish, a writing professor at Northwestern University. Standish confesses:

> I used to think it was one of the world's dumbest ways to spend time, right in there with ice fishing and seeking political office. Once I started doing it, I thought, wait a minute, there's all these other ancillary rewards. I just sort of landed on (mindfulness) myself.
>
> This dumb birdwatching has altered my focus from the usual safe middle distance. Paying attention to birds in the city lets you see more, and for me has spilled over into other things. Doing it gives you the habit of looking carefully, noticing details that never seemed to be there before.[9]

Traveling further down a lake berm, I find a place to park beside another mini-lake. Sitting quietly on a granite rock, I gaze at the empty surface. Within fifteen minutes a few birds cautiously alight on the water. A few minutes later a rush of hundreds are landing at the same spot. I am barely breathing now, don't want to make a sound. My senses are alert. After recent cataract surgery, I do see shapes and colors more vividly. I don't need to know what kind of birds they are, but I want to actively pay attention.

I have choices: listen carefully to songs, note colors or behaviors. My efforts at focusing on these birds plants me into the Now. This does have a calming effect; there is a gut-felt titillation. I think the birds are watching me.

A memory flashes in my mind: Saint Francis of Assisi, the patron saint of animals, encountered a flock of bird in some trees beside the road. It seemed to Francis that the birds were watching him expectantly. Francis decided to preach to these birds about the love that God has for all creatures. Some friars who were with Francis wrote down what he said and it was later published as the famous *The Little Flowers of Saint Francis:*

9. Presto, "Birdwatching Is an Easy Way to Practice Mindfulness," https://www.vice.com/en/article/evq457/birdwatching-mindfulness-meditation-benefits-birding.

"My sweet little sisters, birds of the sky," Francis said, "you are bound to heaven, to God, your Creator. In every beat of your wings and every note of your songs, praise him. He has given you the greatest of gifts, the freedom of the air. You neither sow, nor reap, yet God provides for you the most delicious food, rivers and lakes to quench your thirst, mountains and valleys for your home, tall trees to build your nests, and the most beautiful clothing: a change of feathers with every season. You and your kind were preserved in Noah's Ark. Clearly, our Creator loves you dearly, since he gives you gifts so abundantly. So please beware, my little sisters, of the sin of ingratitude, and always sing praise to God."

While Francis said these words, all those birds began to open their beaks, and stretch out their necks, and spread their wings, and bend their heads reverently toward the earth, and with acts and songs, they showed that the holy father (Francis) gave them great pleasure.

The birds waited patiently for Francis to bless them. The birds flew off in all directions bearing this gospel of God's love to share with all creatures.[10]

As I return to my car, take one last look at Owens Lake, I remember how this place was twenty-five years ago: I see the ominous cloud of poisonous dust rising from the dead lake. But then a collaboration of the City of Los Angeles and local Owens Valley activists revived Owens Lake. It now invites you and me to enjoy aesthetic inspiration, communion with nature and spiritual consolation.

10. Hopler, "Saint Francis of Assisi and His Sermon to Birds, Learn Religions," learn-religions.com/saint-francis-assisi-sermon-to-birds-124321.

Chapter Four

Avant Garde Priest
Father Bob Cornelison, Laguna Beach, California.

You do not need to know precisely what is happening, or exactly
where it is all going. What you need is to recognize the possibilities
and challenges offered by the present moment, and to embrace them
with courage, faith, and hope.

—THOMAS MERTON[1]

RAIN BEATS AGAINST THE bathroom window as I brush my teeth before
going to bed. The mirror reflects the crucifix hanging over our bed. I stare
into my eyes in the mirror's reflection. Goose bumps cover my body. A
deep feeling of gratitude flows from my heart, gratitude for almost fifty
years as a priest, gratitude for staying on the right path, whatever that was,
through many twists and turns, dense thickets of despair. Gratitude for
Grace, for the unearned, undeserved, out-of-left-field gift of God's subtle
nudges; gratitude for one man's mentoring of a clueless, wet-behind-the-
ears new priest.

I remember his penetrating eyes behind thick glasses, he was handsome, thirty-four-years old, jet-black hair that matched his cassock. I had
first met Father Bob Cornelison in 1962 on the sidewalk in front of St.

1. Merton, *Conjectures of a Guilty Bystander*, 206.

Mark's Episcopal Church, Altadena, California. I was in high school then. Little did I know that this man would change the course of my life and shape my ministry as a priest.

We were visiting the church as members of the Pasadena High School Key Club, a boy's honorary society. At the time we were doing the rounds of various houses of worship, a different one each month. Last month we had been to an Orthodox Jewish Temple.

Father Bob gave us a smiling welcome and made one of his little jokes that sets strangers chuckling and puts them at ease. We entered the church for the service and sat in the front pew. Do not do this if you are visiting a Roman Catholic, Episcopal or Lutheran Church for the first time. Do not do this! The liturgical calisthenics will throw you off: you will not know when to stand (to praise), sit (to learn) and kneel (to pray). Luckily, I was seated next to my high school English classics teacher, Mr. John Stewart, a rather stern Episcopalian, who coached us through the service.

After that day, I returned to St. Mark's frequently because my new girlfriend happened to be a member of the parish, and that way I could spend more time with her.

The church of 1962 was quite different from that of today. My old friend, Father Richard Parker of Saint Cross Parish, Hermosa Beach, wistfully remembered: "Back in those days, you just opened the front door of the church, and people poured in." That was true at St. Mark's: always filled on Sundays, and plenty of children at Sunday school. But there were other notable differences. The altar was pressed up against the east-facing wall, the priest did almost all the speaking, women wore hats and gloves, and only men held leadership on the vestry/parish council. In the Episcopal Church the language of worship was all *thee and thou*, based on the old Anglican Book of Common Prayer. Spirituality was about duty and tradition, rather than developing the inner life with God, the better to serve the community.

To a Presbyterian like me, the Episcopal liturgical calisthenics were strange but intriguing. Body movement in the Episcopal Church made you pay attention. At Trinity Presbyterian Church in Hastings Ranch, people remained seated in the pews most of the time. Communion would be handed out on trays and there the wine element was actually grape juice. The rubrics of Communion at St. Mark's were something I had to get used to, though I could not take communion there as I was not yet confirmed.

I remember a men's retreat at Mount Calvary Monastery, the Anglican Benedictine community in the mountains high above Montecito and Santa Barbara. The place was packed with men and boys; the monks presenting long lectures on spirituality. The setting was incredible, with expansive views of the California coast. A golden seventeenth-century Spanish reredos framed the high altar which would be enshrouded by a dense cloud of incense as the monks chanted the *Magnificat* at Vespers. Some deep longing within me awakened as the priest elevated the Host in the early morning mass.

And so my experience of church life went: I was young, interested, moved even, by what I found, but it took something of a shock to get my full attention, my investment. It happened one Sunday. We had been following the Civil Rights Movement in my social psychology class at the University of Southern California. On March 7, 1965, in a voting rights march in Alabama, State troopers and county posse men had assaulted the marchers with billy clubs and tear gas. It became known as Bloody Sunday. I can still recall the television images of the violence shown on Walter Cronkite's CBS News: a wounded woman lying helpless on the Edmund Pettus Bridge.

Another march to Selma, Alabama, was being organized, and a call went out to religious leaders throughout the country to join in. The following Sunday, Fr. Bob announced to the congregation that he was going to Selma to march with Dr. King. This was dangerous. I knew that people had been killed at the previous marches. I imagined Father Bob lying on the ground under the television cameras. I was afraid for him. The feelings of the congregation were mixed. I remember some red-faced men huddled together on the patio outside the church at coffee hour, animated in their anger and disapproval of Father Bob. But off he went. Two weeks later he returned and shared his experience of marching with Dr. King, and his own visceral feelings of fear and dread, as they marched through taunting, rock-throwing crowds.

And my life changed forever; something stirred deep within me. I wanted to live my life like Father Bob. As yet a vocation the priesthood was unformed—my family had tutored me all these years to become a pediatrician.

Father Bob Cornelison, c. 1975. Author's collection.

I immersed myself in the life of the parish, teaching Sunday School to a wild bunch of third-graders. If I momentarily turned my back from the children, before I knew it most of the boys would escape through the window. The choir became family to me, as my quivering tenor tried to blend in the anthem.

Father Bob's curate, Father Pat Tomter, was right out of seminary. I still can't believe it to this day, but most Sundays I would go to his home after the Services and hang out with him and his wife. I know from my later experience that this was deep-fatigue time for a priest after a busy week of ministry and several Sunday services. But there I was, on the Tomter's couch, asking probing theological questions. The approachable clergy at St. Mark's fostered my nascent faith.

I applied for postulancy, the first step toward seminary and ordination. But I was rejected, as my life was in turmoil. I spent my last year of college at Baldwin-Wallace College in Berea, Ohio. As it happens, my uncle, Dr. John Trever, was my Old Testament professor there. He was notable as the scholar who first identified the Dead Sea Scrolls as authentic. He urged me to apply for seminary without the bishop's approval and to go to the Pacific School of Religion, the interdenominational seminary in Berkeley, California—right in the middle of the "summer of love!"

There had to be a whole new scene, they said, and the only way to
do it was to make the big move—either figuratively or literally—
from Berkeley to the Haight-Ashbury, from pragmatism to mysticism, from politics to dope. . . . The thrust is no longer for 'change'
or "progress" or "revolution," but merely to escape, to live on the
far perimeter of a world that might have been.[2]

I was not on the normal, approved track to ordination, but inspired
by Fr. Bob's bold social witness, I began seminary in August 1967. Berkeley
was exotic with flower-children parading along Telegraph Avenue, past
headshops, bookstores, and coffeehouses. Across the Bay, San Francisco
was the locus of the countercultural movement.

I arrived at the seminary dorm, opened the front door just as Marty
Murdock was rushing out. He gave me a quick welcome and asked, "Want
to come to a party in San Francisco?"

"Yes!"

Off we went in his rusty grey VW, arriving exactly at the corner of
Haight Street and Ashbury. A live band blasted music from Golden Gate
Park across the way. My heart was pounding. What was happening?

We went upstairs to the second floor of an apartment building. The
door opened to a lovely, long-haired woman with a bright smile. "Hi Marty.
Come on in."

I entered an expansive living room, filled with young ladies and young
men. A bearded, blond fellow sat in the corner playing the guitar.

All the young ladies there were former Immaculate Heart of Mary
nuns who had left the order in Los Angeles after conflict with Cardinal
McIntyre. They now worked as nurses at the University of California Medical Center, San Francisco. And the young men: novices in the Christian
Brothers, a Roman Catholic monastic community. At the geographic center
of the Summer of Love, I found myself at probably the most G-rated party
in America.

The first year of seminary involved working in the community. The
Pacific School of Religion (PSR) was a progressive school, encouraging
and requiring students to do secular field work. Some worked at the Black
Panthers' food bank and community center at St. Augustine's Church in
Oakland. I was assigned to the Urban League in Berkeley, working as
an employment counselor with young African American community

2. Thompson, "Hashbury Is the Capital of the Hippies," *New York Times*, May 14,
1967.

organizers, some of whom would become city council members in Berkeley and Oakland. I remember meeting many African American residents of the neighborhood who were seeking work, trying to survive with dignity and to support a family. That milieu of desperation pushed me to work long hours to secure interviews for the clients.

There were frequent demonstrations against the Vietnam War at the University of California at Berkeley, a few blocks south of the seminary. My fellow students took part in the demonstrations there and at the Oakland Induction Center. At breakfast, I would hear about students who had been arrested the previous day and had spent the night at Santa Rita Jail.

Another semester I found myself in the Clinical Pastoral Education program, which entailed full-time work as a hospital chaplain. On my first day, they assigned me to the ICU, where I helped zip up the body of a patient who had died. Shortly after, I went to the waiting room with the doctor, who spoke with the family about the death. I wore a crucifix around my neck. The man who died had been a postal worker. His wife came up to me, saw the cross around my neck and began to angrily pound my chest, crying "Why? Why? Why?"

As I entered Herrick Memorial Hospital every morning through the ER, I would take a deep breath and pray for God's grace. No textbook or class lecture was going to help me here. I made the rounds to the different units, never knowing what I would encounter when I entered a patient's room. I floated on grace: became a listening presence and learned to pray from deep within my heart, without a prayerbook.

My participation in the CPE hospital program was enough evidence to show that my life had stabilized. I reapplied for postulancy. Father Bob secured quick support from the vestry to get the paperwork going. He went with me to the diocesan office for an interview with the Standing Committee. His gravitas with all those male priests, the "old boys' network," carried the day.

Returning to seminary, I discovered a few weeks later that Father Bob had resigned from St. Mark's to become Rector of St. Mary's Parish, Laguna Beach. He moved with his five children, Leigh, Nina, Katie, Bobby and Eve, and wife Nancy, to a beach cottage overlooking the Pacific Ocean.

To any young person growing up in southern California (especially from my inland hometown of Pasadena), Laguna Beach was the quintessential beach town. It was where many of us went for spring break and in the summer to escape the brutal heat and smog of the San Gabriel Valley.

The secluded coves and expansive beaches had inspired the California impressionists Frank Cuprien, Edgar Payne, and William Wendt.

At the time, St. Mary's was a traditional village church. Father John Houser had been pastor for many years. The expectation of ministry was that the rector would be in the church office for drop-ins, he would do counseling for sacraments, and make pastoral calls at the hospital. It was a tranquil world where, yes, "you just opened the church door on Sunday, and the people poured in."

And just how did Father Bob break into this introverted, conservative culture? "When I came to my interview, I wore my Brooks Brothers suit and Florsheim shoes and I got them to laugh a lot."

St. Mary's might not have changed for decades, but the world outside was a different matter. This was 1968 and America was in cultural upheaval. There was a dark world under the surface of this idyllic village of tanned surfers, art festivals and expensive homes, for Laguna Beach was also the home of psychedelic LSD evangelist Timothy Leary. *Los Angeles Times* reporter David Haldane writes:

> He used to hang out with a group called the Brotherhood of Eternal Love. They'd get loaded, go up to those caves and maybe spend a couple of nights up there chanting to the moon. Whoever wanted could follow Leary up.[3]

The Brotherhood of Eternal Love often could be found hanging out at the infamous Mystic Art's head-shop on Pacific Coast Highway.

The year Father Bob began ministry at St. Mary's, rookie Laguna Beach police officer Neal Purcell was patrolling late at night. Turning into Woodland Drive, just off Laguna Canyon Road he came across a car with its motor running, stopped in the middle of the road. Purcell investigated. It was Leary, his wife Rosemary and teen-aged son John. The car was full of marijuana and hashish. Purcell made the arrest, and it incidentally brought him national attention. Leary received a ten-year prison sentence. The Brotherhood of Eternal Love, "the Hippie Mafia," hired the radical Weathermen Underground organization for $25,000 to help Leary escape from prison and flee to Algeria.

Laguna Beach needed the ministry of Father Bob. He spent more time out of the church office than in it, on the boardwalk talking with surfers, and at Mystic Arts with the hippie youth. As a licensed marriage and

---

3. Neal Purcell quoted in *Los Angeles Times*, March 31, 2003.

family counselor, he established an easy rapport with troubled youth, many of whom were from the old-money families of Emerald Bay and Three Arch Bay. He was one of the founders of the Laguna Beach Free Clinic. He embodied the epithet: "Preach the gospel at all times, when necessary, use words." Father Bob was living out his gospel in the community. As his reputation grew, so did the parish, attracting medical professionals, therapists, and professors from the University of California at Irvine. But seeds of dissent were being sown, soon to yield a harvest of anger and hate—and I was to get tangled in the nonsense.

When I graduated from seminary in June 1970, there were no jobs in the Diocese of Los Angeles for newly-ordained priests. I found some work in construction and in restaurants while I considered my options. Though Fr. Bob wanted me to work with him, there was little money to pay me. Then Doctor Neal and Meredith Amsden invited me to live with them and their four children in Emerald Bay. I would also receive $200 a month for my car payment. That was enough, and I started full-time at St. Mary's in August 1970.

Father Bob said that a new priest needed to know his parish. I should make as many home visits as I could to establish relationships. From that time on, I made home visits a priority—and indeed that would be my priority for the next fifty years. In those early visits I soon heard the voices of dissent: "Father wasn't in the church office when I dropped in last Tuesday," and, "He's spending too much time out in the community and not on church business. Someone saw him hanging out at Mystic Arts!" As it was these parishioners who had welcomed me, I found myself roused to save the parish from Father Bob.

Fortunately, I remembered my seminary church-music professor, Fr. Norm Mealy, warning me: "Brad, when you go to a parish, people will tempt you to be a critic of the Rector. Remember, you are not the Messiah who has been sent by God to save the parish from the Rector." I never forgot those words and the core virtue of professional loyalty. That which was not shared with me in private confession, I would openly share with Fr. Bob. I never criticized him to others. I was direct with him about any differences between us.

The seeds of dissent came into full flower in October 1970. A parish meeting had been called. The Bishop's representative, Dean Gary Adams, a former Nevada congressional representative, presided. The traditionalists were well-organized, led by a local estate attorney. Shrill, angry voices

33

cried out a litany of indictments, mostly about Father Bob's ministry in the community.

Dean Adams let these furious voices beat their drum for an hour. Then he asked to hear from those who found hope in Father Bob's ministry. The articulate, thoughtful, calm voices of many community leaders shared anecdotes about Father Bob's help and effectiveness. Without seeking a direct vote, Dean Adams asked: "Is there anyone who feels the current situation in the parish is hopeless?" The estate attorney rose to his feet, made a final angry statement, and stomped out of the church with a cluster of his minions. The Dean then invited the congregation to stand and pray for the parish and Father Bob's ministry.

From that day, St. Mary's grew as a beacon of service to the community and a congregation practicing Christ's inclusive love for all.

Reflecting on Father Bob's innate leadership in ministry and his mentoring of this young priest, I find understanding in Chris Lowney's book *Heroic Leadership.* Lowney shares Jesuit leadership secrets that include ingenuity, love, and heroism. As to ingenuity:

> Leaders make themselves and others comfortable in a changing world. They eagerly explore new ideas, approaches, and cultures rather than shrink defensively from what lurks around life's next corner.[4]

We followed Father Bob into the dark alleys of drug and alcohol addiction, poverty among the immigrants who worked in the fancy hotels and restaurants, mental health issues and homelessness. He applied his counseling skills, fostering deep relationships in the Laguna community, bridging the chasms between generations, lifestyles, and the rich and the poor. He taught me that the church must be flexible and adaptable in meeting the needs of the people as those needs presented themselves

I worked with Father Bob in developing the resources of St. Mary's extensive parish property to serve the community and to generate innovative programs, which included: Human Options, a comprehensive program and shelter for abused women; a day-labor center; senior housing; the Friendship Shelter, which housed and provided resources for homeless people; an alternative school for creative high school students; resettlement housing for two Vietnamese refugee families; and drug and alcohol recovery

---

4. Lowney, *Heroic Leadership*, 29.

programs. All these attempts at putting the Gospel into practice flourished; some are still growing, many years later.

Father Bob and I tried to involve some of the more traditional local churches in these community programs but we were told, "First, we want people to be immersed in the Word of God. After they know the Word, then we can work with the community."

I suppose such a response is not unusual, but I am reminded of the story of Saint Pachomius, the third-century founder of cenobitic monasticism. Before his baptism he had been a prisoner of war in Egypt. The early church's core ministry was working in the slums and prisons and the local Christians brought Pachomius food and healed his wounds. After several visits, he asked, "Why are you doing this for me?" They responded, "We are Christians. This is what we do." —"Tell me about who you are," he said. And so, the witnessing and teaching began.

Many non-churched people joined us and grew into deep faith in Jesus Christ because of the witness of Father Bob and St. Mary's Church. Surely this is a natural consequence of Lowney's first secret of leadership: ingenuity. About his second, love, he has this to say:

> Leaders face the world with a confident, healthy sense of themselves as endowed with talent, dignity, and the potential to lead. They find exactly these same attributes in others and passionately commit to honoring and unlocking the potential they find in themselves and in others. They create environments bound and energized by loyalty, affection, and mutual support.[5]

Fr. Bob shared many aspects of ministry with me equally; he did not sideline me as simply a youth minister or curate, for instance—as many a rector might have, instead he empowered me to act on his behalf. Fr. Bob was someone I came to love and with whom I honestly shared my struggles. It was easy to be loyal and trust his leadership, it was easy for me to find Lowney's third secret, heroism, in the way Father Bob led.

> Leaders imagine an inspiring future and strive to shape it rather than passively watching the future happen around them. Heroes extract gold from the opportunities at hand rather than waiting for golden opportunities to be handed to them.[6]

---

5. Lowney, *Heroic Leadership*, 31.
6. Lowney, *Heroic Leadership*, 33.

In the 1970s, Holy Week, between Palm Sunday and Easter Day, was the traditional spring break, when hundreds of young people and college students flooded Laguna Beach. The musical *Jesus Christ Superstar* was on Broadway, the soundtrack to the became a hit record album. Father Jim Friedrich, from Cathedral Films, an inspired genius of visual media, developed a slide-show of classical art and contemporary images integrated with the entire soundtrack of the musical—this was before the movie had been made. On Good Friday night, I positioned a giant projection screen in the sanctuary. Father Jim had two slide-projectors with filters. We spread word throughout the town and the local head-shops. The church was filled to overflowing with hippies with long hair and jingling beads, fragrant with incense, and most of these folks had not been in church for years. And here they were, thoroughly enjoying a presentation of the Passion of our Lord Jesus Christ on Good Friday via a Broadway musical.

Every Good Friday evening through the 1970s, we presented a different film based on the gospel of Jesus, including *Godspell*, Pasolini's *Gospel of Saint Matthew*, and the *Greatest Story Ever Told*.

There are no outcasts—this lesson was hammered home for me during that seminal decade.

> There is neither Jew nor gentile, neither slave nor free, nor is there male and female, for you are all one in Christ Jesus.[7]

Two experiences at St. Mary's Church changed my perspective on the Episcopal Church forever.

On July 29, 1974, eleven women were "illegally" ordained priests by three bishops in Philadelphia, PA, two years before the Episcopal Church would officially authorize ordination of women. A month later, while Father Bob was on vacation, one of these new priests, the Rev. Carter Heyward, visited friends in Laguna Beach. Some women approached me to ask if she could celebrate Eucharist at the Thursday healing service. Looking back, it is hard to engage with whatever hesitation I had about that. I needed time to think about it. I did say yes and attended the service. The Rev. Hayward celebrated the full liturgy. It was not up to me to think or feel this way, but I remember experiencing her competency and priestly authority at that service. The Anglican Communion continues to struggle with this movement of the Holy Spirit.

---

7. Galatians 3:28.

Later, when I became Rector at Messiah Parish, Santa Ana, I made it my mission to recruit and empower other women priests to work with me as equal colleagues. I know that the successful growth and enrichment of that parish was due to the ministry of those six women, all of whom became rectors on their own, including one bishop.

A year later, in 1975, a young man called me and asked if I would do some couples' counseling. I agreed. After a few days the young man appeared in the church office with another man, his partner. Laguna Beach had been a welcoming community to the LGBTQ community for decades. This counseling allowed me to start becoming more deeply engaged with gay people.

We had several sessions together, working on conflict management. What has stayed with me ever since is my impression of the couple's long-time commitment, care, and love for each another. Surely, God was working and present within the love between these two men.

By 1975, Father Bob had been rector for seven years. Remarkably, many of the conservative traditionalists who had stomped out of the church in October 1970, had returned. The estate attorney become the clerk of the vestry and parish council. The parish welcomed this diversity of voices and values.

A few years later, a matriarch of Emerald Bay, a vocal opponent of Father Bob's ministry with troubled youth, drug addicts, and mentally ill people, would herself graduate with a degree in marriage and family counseling. For many years, she led a non-profit that provided services to the very population that previously had been anathema to her.

These experiences crystalized a vision I had of what the church must be: an inclusive community in Christ, where there are no outcasts.

Jesus gives us a radical vision of the kingdom of God: there should be no liberal or conservative, white or person of color, new or traditional, feminist or antifeminist, pro-life or pro-choice, Democrat or Republican or any other ideological pocket that should matter in terms of who is welcome and who can be part of the church.

Ron Rolheiser, President of the Oblate School of Theology, reveals:

> The task of church is to stand toe to toe, shoulder to shoulder, and
> heart to heart with people absolutely different from ourselves—
> but who, with us, share one faith, one Lord, one baptism, and one

God who is Father and Mother of all. To live and worship beyond differences is what it means to have a bosom that is not a ghetto.[8]

I shared ministry with Father Bob for eleven years. Many people told me that was too long; I should have moved on to my own parish before then. But I was choosy about where I wanted to go; the Spirit had not grabbed me yet. But the physics of human relationship took their natural path. For mentor and pupil, that often means a fracture in the relationship. I felt that tension building up for the last two years. It got nasty sometimes. But the Spirit spoke, and I was led to a declining parish in downtown Santa Ana, fifteen miles away. What had once been an affluent supply-town for surrounding cattle ranches had become a densely-populated, Latino-dominant urban center. The church was on the verge of becoming a mission—a congregation financially dependent on the Diocese of Los Angeles. The leadership knew that they had to engage with the surrounding community if the parish was to have a future. Given my education with Father Bob about becoming a spiritual lighthouse to the city, and a church where there are no outcasts, I was the right person at the right time for the Santa Ana parish.

Father Bob and I had little contact for several years. In his retirement, he entered an alcohol recovery program. The Twelve Steps became an essential complement to the gospel of Jesus Christ. Father Bob ran a sober-living home that guided and supported many people into recovery.

A week before he died, I visited Father Bob at his home. I stood at the side of his bed. That beautiful smile was there and the penetrating eyes within a frail body. I held his hand, reminding him I loved him. It was brief, as I kissed him and said, "Bob, I will see you again on the other side."

8. Rolheiser, *Holy Longing*, 131.

Chapter Five

Subversive Spirituality
Pastor Georg Nüglish, Magdeburg, East Germany

The followers of Christ have been called to peace. . . And they must
not only have peace but make it. And to that end they renounce all
violence and tumult. In the cause of Christ nothing is to be gained
by such methods. . . His disciples keep the peace by choosing to
endure suffering themselves rather than inflict it on others. They
maintain fellowship where others would break it off. They renounce
hatred and wrong. In so doing they overcome evil with good and
establish the peace of God during a world of war and hate.

—DIETRICH BONHOEFFER[1]

MAY 1980. A RUSSIAN army officer in full dress uniform sits on the bench
of the boarding platform of the Hauptbanhof, the train station in Magdeburg, East Germany, the Deutsche Demokratishe Republik (DDR). Sitting
on either side of him are his twin daughters, perhaps seven years old. Each
girl has large, bright yellow ribbons tied in her hair. They make a lovely
picture, but the officer looks unhappy. I am guessing Papa is mourning the
end of his posting in East Germany where food and consumer products are
more plentiful than at home. I want to take a photograph, but that is illegal.

1. Bonhoeffer, *Cost of Discipleship*, 65.

I am traveling in East Germany, after a week in Braunschweig, West Germany, researching an article I am writing for the Jesuit magazine *America*. I want to contrast the vitality of the West German Lutheran Church with the Lutheran Church in East Germany.

I am visiting Magdeburg, Leipzig, Dresden, and Erfurt—all in the East, and this requires careful advance work. I had to secure a visa from the German Democratic Republic and to reserve hotel rooms. I am to travel alone and have been warned by officials against deviating from the itinerary.

After checking in at the Hotel International, I go for a walk to purge the melancholy mood descending on me. Standing on a bridge across the mighty Elbe River, I focus on the rippling wakes of passing ships. The butterfly feelings in my gut tell me something important is about to happen— or is it simply the anxiety I feel on this first of day living in the restrictive, suppressed country I have entered?

I remember the feelings and the alien atmosphere as though it were yesterday. Some images stay with you your whole life—perhaps anxiety heightened my awareness, perhaps. . . I took a breath and made up my mind to make the best of my time in Magdeburg.

I wandered toward a war-ruined church, the result of British bombing that destroyed most of the city on January 16, 1945. I passed the ruin and came upon another parish church, war-scarred but rebuilt. And here there was a strange sight: a cluster of college-age people waiting in front of the church.

Curious, I approached the group. I noticed a large poster on the bulletin board announcing the *Evangelishe Studentenvereinigung* (Evangelical Student Union). I asked a young woman if I might attend. She disappeared into the church. I was turning to leave, when I saw a short, stocky man with a concerned look on his face walking toward me.

He wanted to know why I was there.

I introduced myself as a professor of philosophy at a college in California, being careful about my priest identity. He greeted me with a formal Prussian bow, shook my hand, and smiled warmly. Pastor Georg Nüglisch. He guided me by the arm upstairs into the church meeting-room where he presided at a Wednesday night seminar as pastor to the university students of Magdeburg. He had the largest university student group in East Germany.

A dozen tables had been bunched together to make a square, providing seating for a hundred students. Feeling the energy of these young people, I found a seat near Pastor Georg and he began the evening with a prayer. Then he introduced a Roman Catholic priest from Karl Marx Stadt (old Chemnitz) who presented a lecture on the Marxist and materialist elements in the Gospel of Matthew.

After the lecture-discussion, Pastor Georg introduced me. The students' faces lit up when they heard "California" and "America." I was an unusual visitor. I stood up and a barrage of questions hit me: there was concern about America's gluttonous consumption of energy and food resources. I responded with information about church-sponsored programs that promoted responsible stewardship.

Other students probed me with questions about racial justice in America and the oppression of African Americans. Marxists see race and class struggles to be interchangeable issues. The example of Black Americans demonstrated the dialectical conflict between the "haves and have nots" as being still prevalent in society.

I remember my response:

"Racism against Black Americans is imbedded in American Culture. I have experienced this in my own family. My parents are loving parents, but they have strong opinions against Jews, Black Americans, and Roman Catholics. I know that I have experienced and viewed reality through the limited lens of White privilege. My journey away from my family-rooted prejudice has led me to deep friendships with persons of color who are my neighbors, fellow students, and fellow workers."

I told the students how I saw the struggle for life within a Black neighborhood, when I lived in South-Central Los Angeles during the Watts Uprising of 1965. I saw the violence, anger, and police brutality. We had hoped for progress with the Civil Rights Movement, but racial prejudice was still there.

I continued, "I live in a country with freedom of the press, freedom of speech and freedom of assembly. These are hopeful tools for transformation and social justice. The first steps are for White Americans to recognize the lens of our privilege, to confront the culture of racism in which we have been tutored, and to look for opportunities for friendship and relationship with persons of color. I am hopeful."

At the end of the seminar, the students adjourned to the beer cellar in the church. A student grabbed my arm and guided me to join the group. We sat at small tables set up over old beer barrels. The light was dim, and the atmosphere *gemutlich,* cheery, comfortable.

Pastor Georg stood beside me with his hand on my shoulder. He was pleased to have me there and assured me that no question or statement was out of place. The students opened up about their university studies. Most of them were studying heavy engineering (although most had not heard of Caltech or the Massachusetts Institute of Technology).

Several students shared with me their own litany of frustrations of life in the DDR, the poor quality of goods, automobiles which self-destruct after a year's use, and the frequent long lines to purchase goods.

Most of the students came from families of practicing Christians. I remember one young man saying to me, "When I graduate, I will have to make a decision: if I want to have a good professional position, I cannot be a visibly active Christian."

The next morning Pastor Georg gave me a tour of the old church which had been built by French Huguenots, persecuted Christians who did much to build up Prussia during the reign of Frederick the Great in the mid-eighteenth century. The back, unrestored part of the building served as an art gallery.

Pastor Georg shared, "Restoration of churches in the DDR is paid for by gifts of hard West German currency to the DDR," said Pastor Georg. "The Cathedral in Berlin was destined for demolition, but soon monies from West German churches came pouring in, and the church was saved."

Over coffee, he said with pride that his weekly student meeting is the largest Evangelical Student Union in East Germany. He took out a file and showed me the planned seminars for the coming year.

"I will be giving a lecture on Ernst Bloch, a philosopher with a moderate critique of Marxism. The bishop has supported me on this, and I will go ahead, even though it pushes the limits of what the state deems acceptable. We are supposed to study within non-critical limits. Visiting pastors from the West bring in the latest writings in theology. I want these students to know something more than what they get at the university. We are not allowed to counter the sophisticated critiques of Christianity by the Marxist materialists, but at least I have the opportunity to instill some process of critical thinking into the students."

I asked Pastor Georg, "What would happen to you, should you step over the line of permissible behavior and become known as a radical critic of the Communists?"

"I could be sent to Bautzen, a most severe political prison camp near the Polish border, but I doubt that," he responded. "The authorities most likely would send me out of the country."

The next day, I drove with Pastor George, his wife Ursula, and young son Sebastian, to the north for a day in the country to visit the walled medieval town of Tangermünde.

They admired the Mitsubishi Colt I was driving as if it were a Mercedes limousine. As we drove on country roads, a traffic policeman on a white motorcycle shadowed us for a long time. My Dutch license-plate tagged me as a Westerner, a target for speed-trap fines that had to be paid on the spot. We passed three hundred Russian soldiers marching in full battle gear along the highway, as T-80 tanks climbed over distant hills. We were sixty kilometers from the East-West border. If there ever was to be a Warsaw Pact invasion of the West, it would be launched from this area.

We drove past a former Nazi concentration camp hidden in a dense forest, yet clearly marked by the Soviets as a memorial against Fascism.

"We knew of the concentration camps, "Pastor Georg said. "Our Jewish friends were being taken away. There were isolated strikes in factories. We have the same situation today. Someone is taken away by the Stasi, and they go to Bautzen Prison. Many are never seen again. Who knows? Who dares ask?"

His voice grew more intense. "I have seen students taken out of our meetings. I know of young people in my parish who have been brutally beaten by the police. You know what happened: you see the wounds and bruises. But what can you do?"

At Tangermünde we walked through the thousand-year-old walled city gate. We enjoyed *mittagessen* on a ship anchored in the river Elbe outside the city gates. Little Sebastian was excited to be there.

How odd were my feelings as we said goodbye late in the evening in front of my hotel! These persons who were unknown to me two days earlier had shared with me the frustrations and hopes of their lives as I had shared my own life with them. Here we were saying goodbye. They were convinced we would never see each other again.

A week later I was visiting another pastor in West Germany. His parish was the largest Lutheran church in the community. He was an immaculately-dressed, elegant man of about forty-five. His office bookshelves were filled with all the current theological books.

This pastor had two-thousand people in his parish, but fewer than two hundred came to church with any regularity. The German church receives nine-percent of every tax bill paid by each German citizen. The fact that almost everyone pays the tax brings the sum to millions of Deutschmarks, nowadays Euros.

I received more insight into the West German parish situation from a director of Christian education outside Braunschweig. His evaluation of the typical Western pastor was that, after many years in the university, he is highly educated in philosophy and clerical studies, but has been given little experience in practical theology. His own programs were trying to make up for this by providing practical training in preaching and pastoral counseling.

Entrenched in a parish, the Western pastor can be there for many years. His sermon usually consists of philosophical lectures since not a few of these men chose the study of theology because the medical and law schools were full. They can live well (in 1980) on an income of $35,000 a year, housing provided, and make a satisfactory life for themselves studying philosophy and theology.

As my main, original intention in this journey was to contrast the Church in East Germany with the West German Church, I was surprised at the result. I had discovered that the vitality of the church is most strongly felt in a milieu that lacks state affirmation and state support and where there is a struggle for survival, where the cost of discipleship is experienced with intensity.

May 1981. Janice and I have been traveling for the past fifteen days through what seventy years ago was the Austro-Hungarian Empire, visiting Vienna, motoring alongside the Danube to Budapest, into Czechoslovakia: Brno, and Prague. Few people from the West travel in a private car in these countries behind the Iron Curtain. We have been shadowed by local police and secret police, and everything we have said in our hotel rooms has been bugged. I can use my German to communicate, as that was the dominant language in these countries until 1945.

We left Prague that morning, passing through vast, lush farmlands. The road made a slow but steady climb into the dense green forests of the Lusatian Mountains. Under surveillance, we entered East Germany, driving on to Dresden, a city still very much in ruins after the infamous Anglo-American bombing of February 13–15, 1945.

We were following in the footsteps of the reformer Martin Luther, visiting Erfurt, where he was an Augustinian monk and had his life-changing enlightenment about grace as it is presented in the Epistle to the Romans. We toured the castle of the Wartburg where Luther, under the protection of Frederick the Wise, translated the New Testament from Greek into German, and threw a bottle of ink at the devil.

We were stopping in Magdeburg to visit Pastor Georg and Ulla. It had been a year since I had seen them. The door to their home opened. Georg and Ulla greeted us as old friends, meeting Janice for the first time. Janice and Ulla found a common connection in their hospital nursing. We walked to dinner at the Hotel International where we were staying, passing a former Luftwaffe officer's compound. Looking over the wall, we could see laundry hanging from windows and piles of trash.

"Look what those Russians have done to this place," exclaimed Georg. "They live like pigs. This was once a lovely complex. Now the buildings are falling apart!"

Georg's loud complaints made me nervous. I thought we would be arrested.

Georg walked beside me on the street leading to our hotel; Janice and Ulla, arm in arm, sauntered behind. We entered the edifice, heading toward the restaurant to the right of the lobby. A burly man in a dark suit and holding an armload of menus blocked the way. He whispered to Georg: "What are you doing here? You should not be here!"

"*Alles in Ordnung*—everything is okay," I responded. "They are our family." This restaurant was off limits to DDR residents. It was only for visitors, who paid in hard Western cash, and government VIPs. I showed my hotel room key to him.

Yes, we had entered a special world of privilege: plush green carpets, live piano and violin music. The host guided us to a prominent table against a back wall with a wide view of the tables surrounding us.

As I studied the menu, I flashed back on the three weeks Janice and I had spent in Budapest, Prague, and Dresden. When there was food available in a local market, people lined up for fatty sausages, brown-wrinkled oranges from Cuba, shriveled Bulgarian beets, and a strange meat mélange of "parts" that looked like a giant baloney, sliced to order.

This menu revealed a world of dreams: fish, steaks, Italian pasta, and fresh vegetables. Georg and Ulla ordered the beef steak. Georg had a whisky.

"How is your ministry going with the university students?" I asked Georg.

"Last month we began peace demonstrations at the cathedral every Monday evening," he responded. "We call them 'Peace Prayers.' It is a small crowd; many of the students were hesitant at first. After prayers in the church, we march through the main street past the *Bahnhof*."

A flash of hope-filled energy brightened Georg's eyes as he spoke about this movement for political change. His parish and the cathedral hosted groups that actively protested Communist Party policy. He felt compelled to preach stronger sermons against the oppressive policies and action of the DDR.

"Isn't that dangerous: public demonstrations that could be perceived as critical of the government?" I asked.

Pastor Georg responded, "The Church is the only voice permitted to speak critically and openly about the government. We know the Stasi secret police come to these meetings and the peace demonstrations. They take photos and write down names. Participants can receive threatening phone calls and harassment at the university or at work. But the church is the only place in the DDR where one can speak freely."

I asked Ulla, "How do you deal with threats and harassment? Do you feel more fearful about what the government might do?"

"We have lived with this for many years," she said, "especially as the family of a Christian pastor. When I was sick in the hospital, they put me in isolation, cut off from contact with other patients. You remember that our daughter graduated from gymnasium, the high school, last year at the top of her class, but she couldn't go to the better universities."

"Where do you find the spiritual strength to push ahead like this with these demonstrations and what reactions they could spark?" I asked.

"We pray the psalms every night. God is our refuge and strength, a very present help in trouble. The Word of God is our ballast. There is powerful solidarity with others, including non-Christians, who hope for a better, freer Germany.

It was a lovely, surrealistic, evening with our East German friends. The food was the best we had eaten in a month. But there was an anxious ache in my gut. I was afraid for Georg and Ulla. I knew about the brutalities of the Stasi. I also identified with the urgency of the pastor's public witness and the hope for change.

Janice and I walked Georg and Ulla back to their home through the quiet, dark streets. Spring flowers scented the night air. I was grateful for this reunion with our friends, knowing we might never see each other again.

I lost direct contact with Ulla and Georg until 1989 and the fall of the Berlin Wall. I had sent carefully-worded letters to them, but knowing that any such letter would have been steamed open and read by the Stasi agents, I suspect that my letters were trashed.

As I composed this chapter, I have been back-filling information I could find about Pastor Georg and the Peace Prayers movement. What I discovered was that these parochial gatherings and demonstrations became the seeds for much larger demonstrations leading up to the opening of the Berlin Wall and deconstruction of the DDR. Recently, I found a resource that revealed the important peace work that Pastor Georg continued after my last visit:

> The working groups for peace and ecology were founded in Magdeburg under the student pastor Georg Nüglisch. They established networks with other activist groups. They took part in the environmental meeting in September 1981 in Halle and in November 1982 in the working meeting of the ESG (Evangelical Student Association) peace groups. Nüglisch also disseminated the Ten Theses on Possibilities for Nonviolent Actions.[2]

Pastor Georg's grassroots work with his student ministry and peace activism linked with other student groups in the DDR, grew into a popular movement drawing in hundreds of thousands of citizens in massive demonstrations. John S. Conway summarizes this liberation process:

> The churches' courageous stand against political corruption and the misuse of power was hailed as a significant factor in undermining the credibility of the regime. So too was the readiness of church-led 'basis groups' to challenge the ubiquitous secret police, commonly known as the 'Stasi.' These were valiant demonstrations of the popular demand for fundamental rights to freedom of expression, and for liberation from the oppressive structures which had for so long characterized the Marxist-dominated society. The image of a small indomitable band which refused to bow the knee to Baal, but instead defied the might of the all-powerful atheist state, received widespread acknowledgment and approbation. A

2. Neubert, *Geschichte de Opposition*, 466.

large banner paraded through the streets of Leipzig said it all: *Kirche, wir danken dir!*[3]

In 2020, Germany celebrated its thirtieth anniversary of reunification. There is a renewed popular regard for the Christian churches in German and their prophetic voice amidst new struggles for peace and justice.

> One Berlin pastor put it, "We can't just say, 'Now we'll be pious again.'" The church cannot afford to change its character as a forum for thought and political or social innovation. It must continue its role as public educator and must endeavor to continue its role as a dialogue partner to the government on behalf of the people. Perhaps most importantly, said the same Berlin pastor, the church must not stop being "the speaker for the weak." "After all," he said, "that's what we've always been."[4]

---

3. Conway, *'Stasi' and the Churches*, 725.
4. Harris, *Revolutionary Church?*, 34.

Chapter Six

The World's Best Cup of Coffee
Memories of East and West Berlin

The man who fears to be alone will never be anything but lonely,
no matter how much he may surround himself with people. But the
man who learns, in solitude and recollection, to be at peace with his
own loneliness, and to prefer its reality to the illusion of merely natural companionship, comes to know the invisible companionship of
God. Such a one is alone with God in all places, and he alone truly
enjoys the companionship of other men, because he loves them in
God in Whom their presence is not tiresome, and because of Whom
his own love for them can never know satiety.

—THOMAS MERTON[1]

JUNE 2016. I AM traveling the Autobahn toward Berlin with our daughter
Katie. We left our hotel in Braunschweig this morning after a five-day reunion with Ernst Heimbs, Jr., and his family. After thirty miles, I see the
familiar sign "Helmstedt/Marionborn," and a visceral discomfort rises in
me as I remember how I passed through here several times in 1966, trans-
porting Heimbs Coffee to West Berlin.

1. Merton, *No Man Is an Island*, 241.

49

This was Checkpoint Alpha. I remember leaving the reassuring sight of American and British soldiers behind, then the freight truck would enter an intimidating space of high fences, watchtowers with floodlights and East German soldiers with machine guns. We stopped the truck beside the inspection yard. Guards opened the back of the truck to inspect the coffee while I went into the building to present invoices and my passport.

After the guard gave the *Alles in Ordnung* (okay), we proceeded on the Autobahn through the German Democratic Republic, 115 miles to West Berlin. There would be a rest-stop halfway to Berlin where we stopped for coffee and a snack and to relieve ourselves in the woods. That is where the Communist East German tick embedded itself in my leg. I removed most of it when I arrived in West Berlin, but too late, the bug would give me night fevers for weeks and weeks.

As Katie and I passed the still-standing guard towers into the now unified and free Germany, I saw another sign designating the old Checkpoint Alpha as a memorial to those dark days of division and the Wall.

It was fifty years ago, June 1966, when I arrived in Braunschweig for the first time. A family friend had secured a summer job for me with her cousin Herr Carl Heimbs, as a way of furthering my study of German.

When I arrived, I was in a cloud of deep despair. My application for postulancy to begin the process toward priesthood in the Episcopal Church had been denied and I had been dismissed from the University of Southern California in Los Angeles for misconduct: I had stolen books from the University library, which meant that I lost my full-tuition scholarship. But I had planned this trip for the past six months and so I arrived in this north German town where I seemed to be the only one around who spoke English. Twenty-two years previously, October 15, 1944, RAF Bomber Group Five destroyed 90% of the medieval heart of Braunschweig. When I arrived, the city was still a waste of rubble—and my own life was in ruins.

Herr Heimbs reserved a room for me at the local YMCA (CVJM *Gesamtverband*), a tiny space with a bed, card table, chair, and a washbasin. It reminded me of the monastic cells at Mount Calvary Monastery in Santa Barbara. I had rarely been alone like this. I usually had a roommate at home with my brother or in the dormitory at USC.

My return ticket was for mid-September, three months distant. In this town that I had never heard of, I had no access to TV, radio, or telephone to distract or console me. I had uprooted myself and had been planted in this strange place. The Dark Spirit was strongest at night, reminding me of the damage I had done, the hurt I had caused, and the possibility that when I returned, I could be prosecuted for grand theft and sent to jail.

I woke up at six every weekday to work, going downstairs to the dining room. White-jacketed servers brought a soft-boiled egg, wonderful fresh *brotchen*, Heimbs *Kaffee* and juice.

Every morning seemed to be misty and dark, as I walked toward the Oker River, which surrounded the medieval center of the city, its protective moat. Past an ancient water-mill, I strolled up a path through the park, near the burned-out ruins of Alfred Löbbecke's mansion (he came from an esteemed banking family that funded the Franco-Prussian War and served as the private bank of the Duke of Braunschweig). The city would be waking up with clouds of diesel smoke from delivery trucks and Mercedes automobiles. To this day, when I smell diesel exhaust, I am walking through the morning mist in Braunschweig.

Arriving at the loading dock of Heimbs Kaffee, I would find a blue work apron, climb three flights of stairs, and open the heavy metal door into the coffee-roasting room. The minute I opened that door, warm air heavily scented with freshly-roasted coffee brought my senses alive.

In a pile of fifty-kilo burlap sacks of green coffee beans, I looked for chalk numerals, codes for the type of beans. I had to learn the European style of writing the numerals 1, 4 and 7. I found the right sack, and dragged it toward a large steel grate in the floor. Ripping open the sack, I carefully poured the green beans down into the grate.

I rushed downstairs with the empty burlap bag to the next floor, where I managed eight machines. I attached the bag to a machine. The beans were guided into the machine where a photo-electric cell image of a "perfect bean" matched the beans flowing through that machine. An occasional rush of air ejected a bean of poor quality into a big red bucket. I had to keep a close eye on the eight machines so that each sack of processed beans did not spill over on to the floor. That did happen occasionally, and the *Kapitan*/floor manager would blast me with his anger. I emptied the rejected beans from the buckets into a large steel barrel. They sold these beans every Friday to the U.S. Army of Occupation!

I checked the numerical markings on the sack of processed beans then tied it off securely. Then another worker would carry the heavy sack to another steel grate. There was a recipe for mixing one type of bean with another on which depended the market-grade of the final product.

A rush of hot air lofted the beans through an extensive network of steel pipes hanging from the ceiling throughout this floor of the factory. This was the unique Aeotherm roasting system invented by Herr Heimbs in 1954. The green beans circulated through an indirect-heating air stream, roasted gently, avoiding the hot metal parts. Floating in this hot air, the beans roasted evenly from the outside in. The normal roasting process in the USA involved heating the beans on a hot steel grate. "You Americans burn your beans on those hot steel grates," remarked Herr Heimbs. The Aeotherm process continues to this day, which is why Heimbs Kaffee is the gourmet coffee of Germany and I believe to be the "world's best cup of coffee."

If you were drinking coffee in America in 1966, the best taste you could get might well be canned Yuban brewed in a cone filter. 1966 was when Peet's Coffee opened its first store in Berkeley. Peets would school the founders of Starbucks in the art of making fine, European-style coffee.

On the other side of my machines were large tables, where more green beans were hand-sorted. All the people seated there, working carefully and chatting, were persons disabled from the violence of the War. Herr Heimbs was intentional about hiring as many disabled persons as he could.

10 AM. A friendly server in a white service coat would bring me, on a silver platter a *kannchen* of fresh coffee, a cup, and a brown paper bag in which there was a sandwich of German rye bread with thick local butter and liverwurst, made for me by Herr Heimb's housekeeper. They also delivered coffee to my workmates sorting the coffee beans. All was under the scrutiny of the supervisor, Herr Schmidt, about six-feet-four, erect, blond, blue eyes. He must have been a soldier in the Wehrmacht because he shouted orders to us like a military officer.

At noon the machines stopped, and we all went downstairs to the huge dining hall. Everyone was saying to one another *"Mahlzeit"*, which means "have a good lunch." This was my main meal of the day: always a soup or salad, a dish of meat, vegetables, potatoes, followed by dessert. I sat most often with students from the Technical University, who received free lunches. They would not speak much English with me, as everyone was intent on improving my German. A colorful mural filled the main wall of the dining-room, it depicted a Prussian calvary charge in the Franco-Prussian War.

On Tuesday and Thursday afternoons there was a solemn procession of some of the company management toward the *Probzimmer*, testing room, where coffee beans would be tasted, and orders made. One day, Herr

Heimbs invited me to join them. I walked into a long, narrow room with glass windows and doors. Small envelopes of coffee samples from plantations in South America and Africa lay on the table. Each was opened and individually poured into a small roasting machine, ground, placed in a small beaker with filter, and lukewarm water poured through. A cup of coffee for each sample was placed in line on the table. We dipped our spoons into each cup, sucked in the liquid with some air, and let it roll around in our mouth. We spit the sample liquid into a large spittoon in the middle of the room. No one spoke. Each person had a notepad to record reactions to what they had tasted. At some point, by consensus, they decided on future orders, which could mean many hundreds of kilos of raw beans, all to be shipped in through Bremen.

After a few weeks I began to feel at home in the factory. It was a friendly place where the workers seemed to be well-paid and valued. But outside it seemed I would be always walking home through drizzling rain and dark clouds. The further I got from the factory the more the heavy feelings of loneliness and despair returned.

Instead of going straight to my little cell at the CVJM, I made a habit of visiting St. Andrews Church, a thousand-year-old Romanesque Basilica next door to the CVJM.

Above the side-door I could see the ancient gargoyles that spit out rainwater from the gutters. Delicately carved images decorated the high outside walls: the flight of the holy family to Egypt, the crucifixion of Jesus, and the martyrdom of Saint Andreas. Two tall bell towers marked the west entrance. One of them was for centuries the highest church tower in Germany. Construction of this medieval gem had been funded by affluent local merchants.

Though I visited the church dozens of times in the weekday afternoons, I never saw another soul inside. I would go up to the high altar and sit for an hour every day. In 1944, all that remained of this church after the Allied bombing were charred walls. The roof and interior were gutted; the colorful medieval stained-glass windows exploded. By 1966, the church had been restored with a new roof and plain glass windows, but most of the interior decoration built up over a thousand years was gone. There was a strong smell of new cement and a hint of burnt wood.

The Dark Spirit spoke frequently: "You are a thief, a liar, a complete disappointment to your parents. You lost your scholarship. They have kicked you out of the university, and even the church does not want you.

This is who you really are, do not fool yourself otherwise. Your life as you wanted it to be, is over."

Another Spirit urged me to look around for a prayer-book to center myself. I found one, opened it to the psalms. The text was in the old, formal German, "thee" and "thou" of Martin Luther's translation. I found some psalms that I already knew, used some of the German words to get me on the right track. This is what I found:

> Schaffe in mir, Gott, ein rein Herz und gib mir einen neuen, gewissen Geist.
> Verbirg dein Antlitz von meinen Sünden und tilge alle meine Missetat.
> Laß mich hören Freude und Wonne, daß die Gebeine fröhlich werden, die du zerschlagen hast.[2]

My translation:

> Create in me, God, a pure heart and give me a new, certain spirit.
> Hide your face from my sins and put away all my iniquities.
> Let me hear joy and delight, that the bones that you have broken become happy.[3]

As I read the words aloud, the distance between the original composer and my soul collapsed. This was *my* psalm crying out from this very empty place.

Frequent night fevers began a week after the East German tick infected me and lasted for several months. The fever would rage at night, soaking the bed-sheets. I was in my purgatory; I yielded to the painful muscle aches. This was my punishment. I did not have the sense to seek a doctor.

As I look back on this tough time fifty-five years ago, I can see God's benevolent presence. My life had crashed, and I had come to an unfamiliar land. Communication with home could only be through letter-writing: very thin onion paper that folded into an envelope for airmail. But in Braunschweig I would find seeds of hope and consolation that would set my heart in openness to whatever awaited me when I returned to California.

During those summer months that I spent working and living in Braunschweig, most of the time I felt like a zombie with Novocain injected in my brain. But there were two occasions when I came alive for a while.

---

2. Psalm 51, *Luther Bible, 1545*.
3. Author's translation from the German.

One was at my work in the factory among friendly people with that wonderful incense of roasting coffee.

I was also revived on Sundays. I would meet Herr Heimbs at his home parish, St. Katherine, for the *Gottesdienst*. I waited for him outside the church. When he arrived, he was treated like a revered patriarch. We sat together in his pew as we prayed the liturgy. So many of the hymns were songs I remembered from the Episcopal Church, but here we were singing the original German setting, composed, for example, by Bach.

After church, Herr Heimbs would drive me to his home, a mansion on Fallersleber Tor beside the Oker River. There was a splendid Sunday dinner with wine. I had to learn to pray the grace in German by heart.

Herr Heimbs always took a nap after *mitagessen*. I remember that his son, Ernst Heimbs Senior, brought me to the local airport for an outing with his wife and daughter. We drank a curious but refreshing German summer drink: *Berliner Weisse mit Schuss, Weissbier* mixed with raspberry juice. *Weissbier* on its own is very bitter and dry. We watched wide-winged gliders take off and land. Underneath the wings of each glider was the bright red-and-black logo for Heimbs Kaffee.

One Friday morning, Herr Bergmann and I drove a truckload of coffee to West Berlin and spent the weekend in town. On Sunday morning, I walked up Friedrichstrasse to Checkpoint Charlie, the famous Cold War crossover point into East Berlin. If you saw the 1963 film *The Spy Who Came in from the Cold,* with Richard Burton, the East Berlin I was visiting looked like the backdrop to that movie. I left West Berlin, which was a lively, technicolor world, walked through the intimidating gauntlet of East German border guards, into a stark black-and-white world of war ruins and empty streets. I continued up Friedrichstrasse, which before the war was a densely-populated, busy urban neighborhood. It was now almost devoid of buildings. As I came closer to Unter den Linden, I saw the spire of St. Mary's Church, my destination for the *Gottesdienst*. I entered the church to an organ prelude and found one of the last empty seats at the very back. The church was packed. The people sang the hymns with fervent, energetic voices. This was more than intriguing: I was in an East Berlin church in a communist country where religious participation was discouraged. There was a distinct contrast with the style of worship at St. Katherine's Church in Braunschweig where the hymns were slow and ponderous. There most of the parishioners were senior citizens. But here at St. Mary's, faith and worship were lively, the congregation multigenerational. After the service, I spoke with the pastor.

"Why is it that a church in East Berlin is packed and alive with worshipers, while churches in West Germany are half-empty?"

The pastor responded, "One reason is that most of the churches here in Berlin were destroyed in the war. The East German government is not interested in restoring churches. So, the ones that remain are indeed packed with people."

A young man seemed to be waiting for someone outside the church. He saw me, walked up, and began talking right away. He noticed my accented German, asking if I was English or American, then continued in his own clear English. He was friendly and walked with me, offering information about the area. We walked down Unter den Linden, just in time to witness the changing of the guard at the Neue Wache, the Memorial to the Victims of Fascism and Militarism. The Friedrich Engels Guard Regiment goose-stepped to music from a military band, reminding me of old newsreel films of marching Nazi soldiers.

I remarked to my new friend, "The soldiers seem very much like the soldiers of the old German Wehrmacht."

"Yes, that is true. Here in the GDR, we kept a style of uniforms like the old German uniforms and some of the Prussian military traditions continue. This is a highly disciplined army."

I was being careful in my questions and responses, as he could be a plant from the Stasi, the Ministry for State Security, one of the most repressive secret police organizations to have ever existed. If he had asked me to exchange my Deutschmarks for a generous ratio of East German marks, which is highly illegal, I would know it was a trap. But he did not.

I wanted to see the famous Cathedral. He guided me to the place. We entered the main door and walked into a ruin. The high-domed ceiling over the altar had collapsed in the war. Pigeons flew in and out; a heap of debris lay where the high altar would have been.

My guide brought me to the Pergamon Museum nearby. We entered a vast collection of Middle Eastern antiquities. One exhibit took my breath away: a three-storey- high colorful blue-and-gold ceramic tiled ceremonial Ishtar Gate from Babylon of the fifth century BC. We had lunch in the cellar of the East Berlin Rathaus. My friend said he was a university student, and he told me about his childhood in the ruins of postwar Berlin. He hoped to visit the West some day.

At the end of our time, he walked back with me to Checkpoint Charlie. It was sad to say goodbye. We were both aware of that Wall that separated us. He gave me his address but cautioned me to be careful about what I said in a letter, because the Stasi inspect and read all mail. I wrote to him soon after, but never heard from him again.

How quickly we forget what went before! Perhaps it is not the worst thing. Just one generation later, the students in my college philosophy class looked puzzled as I talked about East and West Germany and the Cold War. To them that history seemed as distant as talking about the American Revolution. I had to give the following basic orientation.

After Germany's surrender, May 8, 1945, Germany was divided into East and West Germany. West Germany represented liberal democracy and was occupied by British, French, and American troops. Soviet Russian troops occupied East Germany and imposed communist ideology. Likewise, Berlin was divided into East and West. The Western sector was administered by French, British and American troops on a rotating basis. East Berlin was the Soviet sector. Due to the significant flight of East Berliners to the West zone, in August 1961, the Soviets and the GDR built a wall around East Berlin to control access in and out of the city. The wall was under constant surveillance by East German border guards. At least eighty persons were shot and killed trying to escape to West Berlin. The autobahn corridor from West Germany to West Berlin was supposed to give access to West German citizens and allied troops. Public protests and changes in Russian leadership led to the opening of East German borders and the fall of the Berlin Wall on November 9, 1989. Germany became a reunited country on October 3, 1990. I must admit, in conversations with my German friends, we never thought that reunification would happen. It was a joyful, historic event.

But back to my seminal, formative time in Braunschweig. Saturdays were a break from work so I spent the day walking the city. Founded in AD 861, the city was ruled by the powerful Henry the Lion, married to the daughter of King Henry II of England. During the Middle Ages, Braunschweig was an important trade center and a member of the great trading-group, the Hanseatic League.

The center of the city, surrounded by the Oker River, had been a picturesque, quintessential medieval German town, with narrow streets lined with the largest ensemble of half-timbered *fachwerk* buildings in Germany—until 1944. As I have said, the bombing gutted much of its physical history. I visited the five sectors of the medieval town: Altstadt-markt, Kohlenmarkt (coal market), Wollmarkt (wool market), Hagen Market and the St. Magnus Quarter. The latter had a few remaining *fachwerk* buildings from the sixteenth century. Each quarter had its own marketplace and a thousand-year-old central church.

Braunschweig had been an early supporter of National Socialism. A coalition of local merchants and politicians facilitated the Austrian Adolf Hitler's qualification for German citizenship, giving him a civil-service appointment. As a German citizen, he could become a candidate for the chancellorship. During the years of Hitler's Third Reich, the cathedral was turned into a National Nazi Shrine and the former Ducal Palace became an SS officers' training school.

When I worked on my genealogy recently, I discovered a family connection to Braunschweig. All my relatives come from Sweden and Norway. My mother's father, Abel Burman, was a graduate of the Swedish Royal School of Music, specializing in piano construction. He came to Braunschweig to work for Steinweg Pianos, later moving to New York City to build pianos for their sister company, Steinway. Perhaps I had some mystical, generational connection with this town that had seen me through a difficult time in my life.

I made several bicycle trips to Riddarshausen, a Cistercian monastery a few miles out of town. The Imperial Abbey was founded in 1145 AD. The architecture is simple and utilitarian, with limited iconography. That austerity must have changed after the Reformation, because the pulpit and baptistry are outstanding examples of ornate woodwork. Surrounding the monastery are ponds that support a bird sanctuary.

The monks left after the Reformation; the abbey is now a Lutheran parish church. Side chapels list the names of dozens of local citizens who died in the bombing of 1944. Hermann Goering had a hunting lodge here.

After six weeks, I noticed that my night fevers were going away and with them the haunting voice of the Dark Spirit. One afternoon in Riddarshausen, sitting on a bench shaded by ancient elm trees, beside a lagoon where hundreds of birds took off and landed on the green-blue waters, a deep feeling of solace and peace settled over me. I realized that after the catharsis of these weeks, Braunschweig had become a foundational spiritual home to me, preparing me to walk into the future of God's grace.

The weeks went by as work in the factory and visits with the Heimbs family lifted my spirits. On my last day of work, I visited Herr Carl Heimbs in his large corner office. As I entered, I noticed an elderly woman in a silver suit sitting in a far corner. I sat in a chair facing Herr Heimbs at his desk, presenting to him a set of Kennedy silver coins. Tears came to his eyes, and he held my hand in a lingering handshake.

He stood up, in that erect, perfect Prussian posture, guiding me toward the lady sitting in the corner. She rose and smiled. Herr Heimbs said, "I want you to meet my dear friend, Ihre Konigliche Hochheit, (Her Royal Highness) Herzogin (Duchess) Viktoria Luise von Preussen.

I bowed, kissed her hand, as was the protocol, and these words blurted out of me;

"*Ich habe viel uber Ihre Vater gestudiert*—I studied a lot about your father."

I had never heard of the Herzogin until that moment. But to help me, she gave me a thick copy of her new book, *My Life as the Daughter of the Kaiser,* telling her life-story as the only daughter of Kaiser Wilhelm II. She married Herzog Ernst August of Braunschweig in 1913 in Berlin, the last grand royal event in Europe before World War I, which began a year later. In the book are several pictures of the royal wedding. Princess Viktoria Luise was the Princess Diana of her time. I could see in the photograph of the wedding banquet the czar of Russia seated next to her and the king of Great Britain across the table. These were the kaiser's cousins, grandchildren of Queen Victoria. Within months they would be at war with one another.

For the next fifteen years, I sent birthday cards to the Herzogin every September, and she always sent me a new photograph and personal letter. Her husband had died ten years before our meeting. Herr Heimbs had taken on the role of her protector and close friend.

After a side trip to visit family in Stockholm, Sweden, I returned to California. USC confirmed that I could not return to school but had decided not to prosecute me. I sold my car to pay for damages.

A week later, I was on an American Airlines flight to Cleveland, Ohio. My uncle, Dr. John Trever, somehow secured my admission to Baldwin-Wallace College, a Methodist college of two thousand students, in Berea Ohio, where he was a professor of religious studies.

I had thought my academic life was over, but I responded to this opportunity with hope in the future, intending to be a serious, responsible student. A professor in the drama department and parishioner at the local Episcopal parish, which I attended, recruited me for a play. The school had an excellent performing arts center. During that last year of college, I acted in a series of plays, including *Richard III, Billy Budd,* and in the month of April I presented a play I had written, acted in Edward Albee's *Sandbox,* and in another play presented by the German department. This last year of college was filled with friendships, serious study, and more exploration of my vocation as a priest. A treasure of this year at Baldwin-Wallace were New Testament and Old Testament classes with Uncle John who was a world-class Bible scholar.

But I will never forget my time in Braunschweig—the place where God's grace came to me, and I visited the town several times over the years.

The trip to Germany and Braunschweig with daughter Katie in 2016 was a fiftieth-year reunion for me at Heimbs Kaffee and with the Heimbs family. With great joy I embraced Herr Carl's grandson, Ernst Heimbs, Jr., his colleague Grete Wallner, his sons Heiner and Peter, and several of Ernst's grandchildren.

Ernst had a medical issue at the time and could not drive, but Katie and I were able to take him to one of his favorite country inns. We passed through a farming village where Ernst lived as a youth during the war. It was from here that he witnessed the bombing of the city in 1944 and the horrific firestorm.

Ernst Heimbs with sons Heiner and Peter, Braunschweig,
Germany 2016. Photo by the author.

After that Katie and I continued on the Autobahn to Berlin, this time to experience a city unified. I brought her to the cathedral, which had been in ruins when I visited in 1966 and 1975. The majestic building was now completely restored in golden splendor. As I sat in a pew and dwelt on my journeys in Germany over the past fifty years, I opened the prayer book to Psalm 116:

> I love the Lord, for he heard my voice;
>   he heard my cry for mercy.
> Because he turned his ear to me,
>   I will call on him as long as I live.
> The cords of death entangled me,
>   the anguish of the grave came over me;
>   I was overcome by distress and sorrow.
> Then I called on the name of the Lord:
>   "Lord, save me!"
> The Lord is gracious and righteous;
>   our God is full of compassion.
> The Lord protects the unwary;
>   when I was brought low, he saved me.
> Return to your rest, my soul,
>   for the Lord has been good to you.[4]

After reading this narrative, my friend and editor, Denis Clarke suggested that I revisit the hero archetype.

Swiss Psychoanalyst Carl Jung studied archetypes, primal figures featured in mythologies and religions throughout the world's cultures, as he explored their presence in the dreams and unconscious revelations of his patients. One prominent archetype is the Hero. Jung writes:

> The hero's main feat is to overcome the monster of darkness: it is
> the long-hoped-for and expected triumph of consciousness over
> the unconscious.[5]

A common image of the hero is one who is fearless, gifted, powerful, and famous. American literature professor Joseph Campbell probed deep into mythology and classical literature to describe the hero's journey, as we find in Homer's Odyssey:

> A hero ventures forth from the world of common day into a region
> of supernatural wonder: fabulous forces are then encountered, and

4. Psalm 116:1–7.

5. Jung, *Psychology of the Child Archetype.* CW 9i, par. 84.

a decisive victory is won: the hero comes back from this mysteri-ous adventure with the power to bestow boons on his fellow man.[6]

I can see what my editor was thinking as I look at the three phases of the hero's journey. First comes departure and separation. The hero leaves the home he or she has taken for granted and goes on an adventure. Then there is the initiation: in a strange land, he or she experiences suffering and ordeals, a major life-crisis. But there are people who will help the nascent hero. The Franciscan priest and desert writer, Richard Rohr, OFM, reflects:

> On this journey or adventure, they in fact find their real problem. They are almost always 'wounded' in some way and encounter a major dilemma, and the whole story largely pivots around the resolution of the trials that result. There is always a wounding, and the great epiphany is that the wound becomes the secret key, even 'sacred,' a wound that changes them dramatically . . .[7]

Finally, there is the return to home, the ordinary world. But the hero has been transformed and carries a treasure of wisdom and spiritual power, which must be shared with others. Do you see this in the narrative I have shared above? I know that when I left home I was lost and thought that my life-dreams had been crushed by my crimes. Returning home from Ger-many and carrying the consolation of the Lord in my heart and leaning on amazing grace, I could walk into an uncertain future with hope.

6. Campbell, *Hero with a Thousand Faces*, 23.

7. Rohr, op. cit., 18–19.

Chapter Seven

Desert Angels of Dunmovin

When a foreigner resides among you in your land, do not mistreat
them. The foreigner residing among you must be treated as your
native-born. Love them as yourself, for you were foreigners in
Egypt. I am the Lord your God.

—LEVITICUS 19:33–34 [1]

BLEAK, STRIPPED, BURNED-OUT SHELLS of rock-walled buildings present
the skeletal remains of the desert ghost town of Dunmovin, California,
on the west side of Highway 395, between Little Lake and Olancha, in the
shadows of Mount Whitney and the Sierra Nevada.

Campers and skiers rush past this forlorn scene as they head toward
the livelier destinations of Lone Pine, Bishop, and Mammoth Lakes. This
was once home to a village of desert dwellers. Ruth and Les Cooper were
whom I call the Desert Angels of Dunmovin.

In 2011, after my first book on desert spirituality, *The Spirit in the
Desert: Sacred Sites in the Owens Valley*, appeared in local bookstores, I re-
ceived a surprising phone-call from Ruth Cooper, the owner of Dunmovin.
She had read a chapter in my book about the settlement and the short-lived
religious community established there in 1972 by Father Enrico Molnar.
Father Molnar was an Episcopal priest. He called his foundation the Order

1. Leviticus 19:33–34.

of Agape and Reconciliation. The small rock houses facing the highway were the hermitages where the individual monks had lived.

In *The Spirit in the Desert,* I wrote about Father Molnar:

> Canon Molnar was an extraordinary person; I remember that he spoke six languages, and took pains to know every saint's first, last, and middle names and where he or she was born and conducted his or her ministry. His illuminated manuscripts were so well executed that you would think they came straight out of a medieval monastery. He had been active in diocesan programs until at one point in his life he began to experience visions of saints and of Jesus, which prompted him to leave institutional ministry and found a religious order. The community began here in Dunmovin and later moved to Chermainus, British Columbia.[2]

As Ruth shared some of her personal story with me from her new home in Ridgecrest, California, my imagination began to place muscle, sinew, and skin over the dry, dead bones of old Dunmovin. I recalled Ezekiel's famous vision of dry bones:

> So I prophesied as I was commanded. And as I was prophesying, there was a noise, a rattling sound, and the bones came together, bone to bone. I looked, and tendons and flesh appeared on them and skin covered them, but there was no breath in them.[3]

With her slight Southern accent, Ruth began to reveal the story of Dunmovin. As she spoke, I could hear the animation in her voice as she reimagined her town once again alive and thriving. In the early 1900s, the place was known as Cowan Station, named for the pioneer James Cowan. It served as a freight station for the silver ingots being transported to Los Angeles from Cerro Gordo, in the Inyo Mountains. Water was piped in from Talus Canyon. In 1936, Charles and Hilda King bought the property and changed the name to Dunmovin. There was a post office here from 1938–1941. Ruth and her husband bought the town in 1961.

There would be several more telephone conversations with Ruth. Each time I could sense that she was reviving her memories of Dunmovin and her beloved husband Les.

Les grew up on a South Dakota cattle ranch, played football at the University of Minnesota, where he studied mining. He went on to be a

2. Karelius, *Spirit in the Desert,* 39–40.
3. Ezekiel 37:7–8.

professional boxer, hunter, storyteller, and a stuntman in Hollywood westerns, including the classic films *Stagecoach,* and *Gone With the Wind.* Most of the westerns that Les worked in (and there were hundreds) were filmed in the Alabama Hills outside Lone Pine. After he broke his back in 1943 he became an attorney and a gold miner.

Ruth and Les married in 1949, settling in the desert town of Ridgecrest in 1952. They had a special heart for mentoring young people. Ruth went to law school herself and became Ridgecrest's first woman lawyer. In 1961, they purchased 160 acres at Dunmovin. Why did they make the move to this isolated little desert village? Ruth suggested there was something spiritual about that windswept place at the foot of the majestic, jagged Sierra Nevada mountains.

Ruth and Les Cooper in their law office, Dunmovin, California, c. 1970.
Photo from Steve Lopardo collection.

Between our telephone conversations, I continued to make retreats to the Owens Valley. Now I no longer rushed past Dunmovin; I would stop and walk about the ruins. Some people still lived there, toward the back in rusting mobile homes. On the frontage property is the shell of a restaurant and Ruth and Les' old home and law office.

As I stood there highway traffic rushed by on the now-divided highway 395. There is always wind here, sometimes so strong as to blow eighteen-wheeler trucks onto their sides. Violent summer rainstorms create flash floods that rush out of the desert canyons and across the highway. There are very few services for fifty miles. 110°F summer heat and hot winds feel like a blowtorch to the skin. Ruth's unfolding memories had given me a haunting, melancholy feeling about a vibrant life that had now passed. Although I promised to visit her at her home in Ridgecrest, I missed the opportunity. Ruth died on April 15, 2019. However, Dunmovin still has life in the fond memories of her family.

Another grace for me was a letter from her nephew, Steve Lopardo. As he was managing her estate after her death, he found my contact information in her address book, sent me her obituary, and we met for lunch.

Les Cooper was a mentor to his nephew, and the best man at his wedding. Steve remembers his uncle's counsel in a book that Steve edited:

> I spent part of the summer of 1965 with one of the wisest men I've ever known, my Uncle Les, a country lawyer who lived in the ghost town of Dunmovin at the foot of the Sierra Nevada Mountains. I was very worried about whether I would make the Junior High football team in the fall, and all other weighty problems 12-year-olds lose sleep over. Les sat me down and shared the best advice anyone ever gave me. He said: "Steve, always remember that happiness is a journey, not a destination." In other words, focus on the moment, and the future will take care of itself.[4]

Steve went on to play football at the University of Notre Dame. And now, over lunch, he breathed more life into the dusty desert bones of Dunmovin and revealed that Ruth and Les Cooper had a special ministry to desert travelers and troubled youth, sheltering the lost and abandoned.

Ruth and Les were desert saints at Dunmovin because they provided a radical hospitality to desert travelers. Highway 395 is a deadly road, where fatigue or alcohol or drugs cause drivers to drift off the highway into horrific rollovers in the rock-strewn landscape. Ruth and Les rescued the injured and helped stranded travelers with food and lodging. But it was their heart for vulnerable young people that stands out. In their home they sheltered abused children and youth.

You may remember that the psychotic cult leader Charles Manson lived with his followers at the Barker Ranch which was a hundred miles

4. Lopardo, *Best Advice*, 2.

from Dunmovin. Manson had a particular attraction to underaged, vulnerable girls who would be inveigled into his cult. If a girl ran away, she could be caught and killed. One young girl did escape and found herself on Highway 395, dropped off by a trucker at Dunmovin. Ruth and Les took her in and hid her for several months as Manson's followers searched for her.

Ironically, Les was assisting Frank Fowles, District Attorney for Inyo County, when Manson was arrested and brought to the County Courthouse in Independence, about sixty miles north of Dunmovin.

The radical desert hospitality that Ruth and Les Cooper provided at remote Dunmovin has powerful roots in Judeo-Christian-Islamic spirituality. As their nephew remembered the compassion of Ruth and Les Cooper, I recalled the Patriarch Abraham and what Saint Theodoros the great ascetic, one of the early desert fathers, wrote:

> Accepting the task of hospitality, the Patriarch (Abraham) used to sit at the entrance to his tent (cf. Gen 18:1), inviting all who passed by, and his table was laden for all comers including the impious and barbarians, without distinction. Hence, he was found worthy of that wonderful banquet when he received angels and the Master of All as guests. We too, then, should actively and eagerly cultivate hospitality, so that we may receive not only angels, but also God Himself. 'For inasmuch,' says the Lord, 'as you have done it to one of the least of these My brethren, you have done it unto Me' (Matt 25:40). It is good to be generous to all, especially to those who cannot repay you.[5]

Abraham, patriarch to Jews, Christians, and Muslims, modeled the foundational virtue of desert hospitality. For Muslims, hospitality is a basic virtue in the Islamic ethical system. Its roots are in the Bedouin value of welcome and care for the stranger in the deadly desert. Of the Arabic word *dayafa*, Mohammed expounded, "There is no good in one who is not hospitable."[6] The Holy Qu'ran emphasizes *karam*: providing food to the needy stranger.

Miriam Shulman and Amal Barkourki-Winter explain:

> The virtue seems an ineluctable product of the landscape . . .
> to refuse a man refreshment in such a place is to let him die, to

---

5. *Philokalia*, Vol. II, 32–33.

6. Prophet Mohammed quoted in *Hosting the Stranger: Between Religions*, 134.

threaten the openhandedness nomadic peoples must depend on to survive.[7]

And the scholar and Buddhist, Snjezana Akpinar concurs: "Hospitality was considered as an act of unconditional surrender to the needs of others."[8]

August 2010. A knock on my office door. The door opens and there is a parishioner, Evangelina. Her normally bright, smiling face is solemn, her voice quiet. She speaks in Spanish: "Padre, I met someone outside the church, and she needs to speak with you. She was sitting on the bench at the bus stop, and she was crying a lot. It frightened me. She is crying about her son Jesus. I do not know her, but I know it would help if she could talk with you."

The sad lady appears, tears welling up in her eyes, her face flushed. She is Latina, perhaps fifty, with a bent back. She cautiously enters my office and I invite her to sit on the sofa. She releases a deep sigh; her body shakes as she sobs.

I am fluent in Spanish, but at times like this, with someone I do not know, I need a context to understand what is being said. Give me a subject, verb, and direct object. Why is she grieving?

Evangelina sits beside her, stroking the woman's back and speaking softly. Her name is Luz Maria. Something has happened to her son Jesus. Last month, July, Jesus was trying to cross the border from Mexico with his uncle Luis. They had found a remote area on the Mexico-Arizona border, a desolate, dry desert. At this time of year, it would frequently be 110°F.

Luis and Jesus had been chased by bandits and had hidden in the dense desert brush: cholla, mesquite, and thorny cacti. But they become separated. After hiding for several hours, believing that the bandits had moved on, Luis called out for his nephew. For several hours, Luis searched that landscape, calling his nephew's name. No response. Travel had to be by night because the scorching heat would return in the morning. They had lost water and supplies as they ran to escape from the bandits. And Jesus was not to be found.

Luis continued the journey, getting to California. A family member picked him up in El Centro and he came to Santa Ana—without his nephew.

7. Schulman and Barkouki-Winter, "Extra Mile," *Markulla Center for Applied Ethics,* https://www.scu.edu/ethics/focus-areas/religious-and-catholic-ethics/resources/the-extra-mile/.

8. Akpinar, *Hospitality in Islam,* 7.

Luz Maria had been waiting for her son to appear for several weeks. Every night she had the same dream: her son was wandering in the desert crying for help. Her maternal instinct to help and protect her son made the dream a horrible nightmare. I could identify with her fear and terror at this dream, as I sometimes have the nightmare that our disabled son Erik is lost somewhere, and we can't find him. This is the worst feeling I can imagine.

Luz Maria said that last week the nightmares became more intense: she could see her son lying dead under a desert tree.

Luis convinced two cousins, who are documented and legal residents, to go to Arizona, to the general area where he was with Jesus, and search for him. By this time two weeks had passed. The Arizona desert heat was 115°F.

On a well-worn trail leading up from the border they found Jesus. He was indeed dead, propped up with his back against the trunk of a mesquite tree. In the intense dry heat, his body was partly mummified. His shoes were missing. There was no water anywhere in that hellish heat.

As I listened intently, Luz Maria forced herself to focus and complete the narrative. Evangelina continued to massage her back. And then the sobs returned, as she repeatedly cried *"Mi Hijo, Mi Hijo*—My child, my child."

I invited her into the church sanctuary. I held her hand as we walked to the dark corner of the Lady Chapel. She knelt before the image of the Virgin of Guadalupe. I lit a blue votive candle and knelt beside her, opening the Prayer Book to the Litany, I prayed in Spanish:

> Deliver your servant, Jesus, O Sovereign Lord Christ, from all evil, and set him free from every bond; that he may rest with all your saints in the eternal habitations; where with the Father and the Holy Spirit you live and reign, one God, for ever and ever. Amen.[9]

I continued praying, but my own body was absorbing Luz Maria's grief and I had to read the prayer slowly, as my own tears flowed:

> Almighty God, look with pity upon the sorrows of Luz Maria. Remember her, Lord, in mercy; nourish her with patience; comfort her with a sense of your goodness; lift up your countenance upon her; and give her peace; through Jesus Christ our Lord. Amen.[10]

At that time of year, the Arizona desert landscape is blowtorched by the incredible heat. Dozens of immigrants die each year for lack of water, as they struggle through the desolate landscape.

9. *Book of Common Prayer*, 464.

10. *Book of Common Prayer*, 467.

If only some compassionate souls would bring water out there.

Less than five miles from the place where the body of Jesus was found, there is a building known as "The Barn" offering food and water to undocumented people crossing the border from Mexico. Since this place of assistance for desperate desert travelers is well-known to immigrants, it is possible that Luis and Jesus were trying to locate it before they ran into the bandits and had to flee.

For many years, concerned volunteers from an organization called "No More Deaths" in southern Arizona have been planting caches of food and water as a help to people walking through this desolate desert wilderness.

Recently, Scott Daniel Warren, who teaches at Arizona State University, was at the Barn aiding two lost, undocumented immigrants. The U.S. Border Patrol had been observing activities there. When they saw Scott helping the two men, the U. S. Border Patrol moved in and arrested Scott for harboring illegal immigrants, providing them with, "food, water, beds and clean clothes."[11]

Scott's attorney, William Walker, said that there has always been an understanding between No More Deaths and law enforcement: "We have always had an understanding here with both the U. S. Attorney's Office and the Border Patrol and also the wilderness area managers that we are a neutral party. We don't smuggle people; we don't violate the law. What we do is help to save lives and they've recognized that for years."[12]

But when Border Patrol agents find these caches of food and water in the desert, they pour out the water on the ground.

In a press release, No More Deaths reported:

> We document how Border Patrol agents engage in widespread vandalism of gallons of water left for border-crossers and routinely interfere with other humanitarian aid efforts in rugged and remote areas of the borderlands.[13]

Officer Carlos Diaz of the Border Patrol office responded after viewing videos of the destruction of the water and food: "Our agents are briefed frequently and are advised frequently to leave those resources alone. If anybody sees any activities like the ones in the videos, they need to inform us

---

11. Silva, NBC News, January 23, 2018.

12. Silva, NBC News, January 23, 2018.

13. Silva, NBC News, January 23, 2018.

so we can take the corrective action because it is not acceptable." At a court hearing, the judge dismissed the charges against Scott Daniel Warren.

For many years, I have been writing about the spiritual potency of the desert landscape. But in the story about Luis and Jesus, we learn that for hundreds of desperate, undocumented persons, this is a life-threatening place—a hellish furnace.

Two contending voices: compassionate volunteers from No More Death, moved by the ancient desert ethics of hospitality; dedicated Border Patrol officers protecting our desert wilderness borders. Toward which voice is your own heart drawn?

Chapter Eight

The Holy Gospel of our Lord Jesus Christ, according to Father Gordon Moreland, SJ.

Jesus performed many other signs in the presence of his disciples, which are not recorded in this book. But these are written that you may believe that Jesus is the Messiah, the Son of God, and that by believing you may have life in his name.

—GOSPEL OF JOHN[1]

The farther the outward journey takes you, the deeper the inward journey must be. Only when your roots are deep can your fruits be abundant.

—HENRI NOUWEN[2]

THE MOST IMPORTANT ADVICE I can give to a man seeking a deeper relationship with God is to work faithfully and consistently with a spiritual director. Spiritual direction is "help given by one Christian to another which enables that person to pay attention to God's personal communication with

1. John 20:30–31.
2. Nouwen, *Inner Voice of Love*, 94.

him or her, to respond to this personally communicating God, to grow in intimacy with God and to live out the consequences of the relationship."[3]

Spiritual direction can help you to explore your experiences of God, discern important decisions, heal trauma from the past, and grow into God's deepest desires for you.

The process begins in your prayers as you listen to God's call for you. Speak with a member of the clergy or someone you know who has been under spiritual direction. Local retreat centers can help you find a spiritual director: someone who has been through a certification program for spiritual direction. Above all, expect that opening yourself up to spiritual direction will take time and commitment.

Spiritual writer and priest Henri Nouwen advises:

> The goal of spiritual direction is spiritual formation—the ever-increasing capacity to live a spiritual life from the heart. A spiritual life cannot be formed without discipline, practice and accountability.[4]

Nouwen believes there are three disciplines that will complement your experience with spiritual direction: the discipline of the heart, the discipline of the book, and the discipline of the church.

The discipline of the heart involves contemplative prayer, inviting God into our total being, including all that has been hidden and secret.

The discipline of the book involves reading the scriptures and spiritual writings. You will find that as you read, the Spirit may connect words and phrases to where you now are in your life, what you are currently seeking and pondering. After I began spiritual direction, meditation on scripture helped me to hear those words in a new way, as if they were written for me.

The discipline of the church will be a challenge for some readers of this book. You may be a spiritual seeker of God, but you may never have had a life in a religious community, or, for some reason, you may have left your community. The problem is that the Christian faith is communal, not solitary, requiring that if we are to grow with God, we need to have life in community. In regular worship in the church, we experience the gospel narratives of Jesus through the liturgical year, an annual calendar of seasons commemorating the life and teachings of Jesus. Our sometimes-messy

---

3. Barry and Connolly, *Practice of Spiritual Direction*, 8.
4. Nouwen, *Spiritual Direction*, xiii.

experience of human relations in a religious community is rich fodder for reflection with a spiritual director.

In our individualistic culture, we can be drawn to the self-reliance of the desert fathers and mothers, how they found a rich spiritual life in their deprivation, silence and solitude. But take note that eventually they found that physical and spiritual survival in the desert required the help of others, and so arose the first Christian monastic communities. It may be ironic, but successful solitude is always dependent on others. In contrast with the iconic New Yorker Magazine's cartoons of the solitary guru living in a cave who is visited by eccentric spiritual seekers, Jesus called a community of disciples to follow him.

Nouwen continues:

> The more we let the events of Christ's life inform and form us, the more we will be able to connect our own daily stories with the great story of God's presence in our lives. Thus, the discipline of the Church, as a community of faith, functions as our spiritual director by directing our hearts and minds to the One who makes our lives truly eventful.[5]

In 1990, my psychiatrist Robert Phillips, MD, recommended spiritual direction for me and sent me across the street from his office, to the Center for Spiritual Development on the campus of the Sisters of Saint Joseph of Orange. I had a general idea about spiritual direction, but little experience. I knew it was something deeper than pastoral counseling. I was apprehensive that someone was going to criticize me about my imperfect life or dictate a curriculum for perfection.

Somehow I ended up with Sister Jeanne Fallon who had recently returned from missionary work in Papua New Guinea. I sensed the fire of God within her. My own life was a frenzy of multi-tasking busyness for the church. God was in the far distance, and Erik was in and out of the hospital. Sister Jeanne's exploratory interview awakened in me the realization and the fear that I was actually trying to *hide from God*. Even after two years of intensive psychotherapy, something lurked in the dark shadows of my consciousness which made me anxious about proceeding.

Since that moment of enlightenment, I have asked many clergy about their spiritual directors: most do not have one or if they do, they see them infrequently.

---

5. Nouwen, *Spiritual Direction*, xvii.

The Spirit urged me to stay with Sister Jeanne. She invited me to begin the *Spiritual Exercises* of Ignatius of Loyola which take a year to complete. During our weekly meetings she guided me through this five-hundred-year-old Jesuit program of daily meditation on scripture and contemplative prayer. This experience opened my heart to the actual presence of Jesus as companion and friend, and the secrets in the dark recesses of my soul came out into the light of God's compassionate love. After I finished the *Exercises,* Sister Jeanne sent me to a Jesuit priest and recovering alcoholic. At that point, I was attending Twelve-Step meetings of Adult Children of Alcoholics, newly aware of long-term compulsions and addictions. I took a moral inventory, admitting to myself, to God and to another human being the exact nature of my wrongs.[6]

I began my confession with this prayer: "Almighty God, my inventory has shown me who I am, I admit to my wrongs, yet I ask for Your help in admitting my wrongs to another person and to You. Assure me, and be with me, in this step, for without this step I cannot progress in my recovery. With Your Help, I can do this."[7]

With this priest, I shared a detailed confession. I had written everything down so that I would not try to evade the hard reality of my past behaviors. It was this priest who sent me on to Father Gordon Moreland, SJ, at the House of Prayer for Priests in the Diocese of Orange, located in the foothills of the Saddleback Mountains.

I remember my first encounter with Father Gordon as he welcomed me at the entrance to a compound of southwestern-styled buildings. As I sat in a chair facing him in his office, the windows behind him revealed a vast desert garden. We shared a common interest in desert landscapes and plants. Over months and years, that chair became a sacred place for encounters with the Lord.

For many years, Father Gordon had been novice master to young Jesuits, fostering their spiritual formation (some of them would become bishops and cardinals). He spent thirty-five of his sixty-nine years as a Jesuit in the Diocese of Orange where he became a revered retreat leader for its priests. In 2021, he moved to the Jesuit retirement residence in Los Gatos, California.

6. Step five in Alcoholic Anonymous is called "Confession", when we "admit to God, to ourselves and to another human being the exact nature of our wrong." This step involves a written inventory of our wrong and should be shared as early as possible in recovery.

7. *FHE Health,* www.fherehab.com.

I remember that my early years with him were filled with tears and anxiety about Erik's health crises, and epithets and curses of anger and frustration about my parish and diocesan ministries. I would arrive with heartache and rage-driven fantasies and leave with a spiritual infusion of God's love and affirmation from Father Gordon. He did not act as a therapist, analyzing my interior life and making prescriptions. In Father Gordon I found a mellow, mature soul to whom I wanted to be accountable. That is something I learned from the Twelve-Step experience: to be accountable for my life and practice bringing everything into the light. As I look back, I believe that as I talked with Father Gordon, I was practicing being real and honest with God. I committed myself to meeting with Gordon every month for twenty-seven years.

The four gospels of the New Testament are presented as eyewitness accounts of the life, ministry, death, and resurrection of Jesus. There are also persons who come into our life as "eyewitnesses" to the living Christ, persons whose deep encounters with the Lord radiate their living faith to us and, by their words and presence, draw us closer in faith and friendship with Jesus. A gospel is an *evangelion*, "good news." Father Gordon Moreland, SJ has been an *evangelion* of Jesus to me.

As I sat with Father Gordon, I always held a yellow legal pad on my lap. I would write down phrases he said, scripture passages, and spiritual reading to be explored later. Writing helped me to listen. From these notes during my last year with Father Gordon, I have gleaned only a small part of "the Holy Gospel of our Lord Jesus Christ according to Father Gordon Moreland SJ," but here are some of the things he would tell me.

God is love and joy. Most people think of God as power, an entity to cope with, to dread, or to hold in awe. Saint Paul shares his own experience of God in the Epistle to the Romans: "May the God of hope fill you with all joy and peace as you trust in him, so that you may overflow with hope by the power of the Holy Spirit."[8]

God is joy. Joy wants to diffuse itself into creation, creating humans who are capable of joy. What God wants from us is joy. Erik radiates that joy to everyone around him. I frequently talked about that nagging critical voice in my head, reminding me of past sins or being negative about people close to me. Gordon's advice: focus more on seeing myself as the Lord sees me. It helps to remember with gratitude moments of joy.

---

8. Romans 15:13.

God is love, personified. God is joy, personified. God is mercy, personified. This creates a new matrix for thinking about God as other than the serious, chastising judge, watching our every move.

Gordon remembers notorious criminals in prayer at his daily mass. For instance, he remembered in prayer Andrew Cunanan, who murdered Gianni Versace in 1997. Father Gordon prayed for him during an early morning mass. He sensed Cunanan's presence, who was so full of guilt that he could not accept the Lord's help. Gordon experienced the blessing of the Lord on his prayer-friendship with murderers and the unfaithful departed. He wants to help them let go of their sins to the Lord and prays that they will experience a surge of joy from the Lord. "You cannot welcome the Lord Jesus if you are still given over to your corporal sins."

As I mentioned, I often arrived at the House of Prayer heart-heavy. Memories of dark, depressing times would rise up and become vividly real again. Was this the work of the Dark Spirit creating resistance to Father Gordon's words of light and hope? Gordon responded: Jesus said, "Whoever follows me will never walk in darkness, but will have the light of life."[9] He shared his memory of the Spanish mystic Saint John of the Cross (1542–91), who knew dark times when he was beaten and persecuted by his Carmelite community for his reforming efforts. Yet, locked up in a dark cell next to the monastery latrine, he wrote the Spiritual Canticle, proclaiming his love of God in dark times. As a teenager, Saint John had worked in a hospital caring for men with syphilis and dementia. He would clean them with such reverence that people were much taken by his servant persona. In John's love for these dirty, sick men, he saw Christ in them. This experience made him aware of God's love.

In my imagination, I see John of the Cross locked up in a tiny, dark room next to the nauseating smell of the monastery latrine. At night, he was in total darkness. His food was bread and water and salted fish. God seemed distant and the fire of his faith was almost out—only embers remained. But the living flame of God's love did not abandon him. Later, when he escaped captivity, the fiery ardor for God rekindled, inspiring the mystical poem *The Living Flame of Love* (circa 1585).

Following on from which, Gordon would always emphasize: "It is so important to be in touch with God's love for us, more than our love for God.—Let yourself be loved by God. Know yourself as beloved.—The Lord

9. John 8:12.

loves me more than I love me. I am safe in His hands.—The Lord loves Erik more than I love Erik. Erik is safe in His hands."

Gordon is far from being a one-trick pony. For instance, he cultivated a deep friendship for China and its people, making more than a dozen month-long trips there, touring the back roads-less-traveled with Chinese friends as guides. He carried in his heart the spirit of Matteo Ricci (1552–1620), the Italian Jesuit priest whose profound missionary work pierced the confines of the Forbidden City to encounter and counsel the emperor, syncretizing Confucian values and traditions with Christian values and traditions.

In his travels, Gordon asked the Lord that he might be a friend to China and waited for confirmation from the Spirit. At the end of one visit, he was at dinner with his friends and several military officers. You can imagine some tension there between the Chinese officials and this lone American. Gordon did not speak Chinese, but his expressive face communicated the love and joy of the Lord. All the people at the table stood, raising their glasses, toasting Gordon: "Welcome to a friend of China." The Lord Jesus seemed to confirm Father Gordon as spiritual ambassador to China. At the end of the evening, he was asked, "What did you think of this evening?"

Gordon responded, "I am a religious man, a Jesuit priest. Before I came to China, I asked the Lord that I could be a friend to China. One thing I am certain of is of God's love for all of us."

One of the military men answered, "On behalf of the Third Regiment, I welcome you as a friend of China!" Gordon told me this story several times, radiating some of the joy he must have communicated at that memorable dinner. The Spirit must have infused the dinner guests with the joy of the Lord, because two men in their fifties approached Gordon as he sat in a car ready to leave. Smiling, they greeted Gordon, saying, "We love you."

There has been a lot of progress in this country of a billion-and-a-half people. Though four-hundred million live on one dollar a day, there is a burgeoning middle-class and indeed more billionaires in China than anywhere else. A systemic command-economy has pulled two-thirds of the people out of poverty in just seventy years. The United States has not been able to do that. We need to acknowledge, even applaud this accomplishment.

Rather than "spiritual direction," Gordon preferred the term, "spiritual conversations." As a teenager working on his family's farm in eastern Washington State, he planted grapevines and learned the art of training two lower branches and two upper branches of the new vine onto a wire trellis.

The trick is to guess which sprouting buds can be encouraged by pruning correctly. If you choose poorly, then your crop will be diminished. Working at vine cultivation requires developing intuition, learning to see how the plant itself wants to grow. The analogy is clear: the task of spiritual direction is to draw out a person's deepest desires.

Another important thing that Gordon left with me was when he referred to the special dignity of the penitent. I remember hearing private confessions at my parish in Santa Ana. Some people carry their sins like heavy rocks in their spiritual backpack. Shame and guilt wear them down. Previous counseling from other clergy often added to the shame of these penitents. When I look back to that spiritual inventory of the Fifth Step with the Jesuit priest, I remember feeling like Lazarus: The Lord had set me free. As I arrived at a Twelve-Step meeting in Dana Point, California, on a dense foggy night. Several men were outside the entrance welcoming everyone, glad that they had shown up. Listening to those testimonies of recovering alcoholics that night, one of whom was at the time a student of mine at the college, reminded me of an Easter Sunday service, but there was more Easter resurrection there than I have ever felt in church.

After Father Gordon moved from the largely Anglo-Northwest to Southern California, on Ash Wednesday, as he imposed ashes on parishioners, he was especially struck by Latinos, and how they would wear the penitential mark on their foreheads with pride. These ashes are not mortification, as taught by ancient theologies: we *glory* in our penance. We are *worth* the blood of Jesus on the cross. It is not that we forgive and forget our sins; it is better to know you are forgiven and to remember your liberation from sin and death. Right now I am remembering how through our many years of marriage, Jan and I continue to learn about forgiveness for each other.

Gordon tells a story about a crooked, bent tree that grew beyond the corner of a house, a "wounded tree," obscured under the lattice of the roof. It worked its way out into the light. The forestry person had pronounced the tree as "broken," but now the tree had become strong, growing to a hundred feet.

From his own life with God, through all the struggles for faith within his own humanity, Father Gordon experienced the love and forgiveness of the Lord. He has lived his evangelion through a radical love for the unfaithful departed, helping them to let go of their sins and to embrace the joy of the Lord. You may ask him: What does God want from us? More obedience, following the rules, spiritual perfection? God wants a relationship with you. The trick is this: *we love because God has given us the ability to love.*

My prayer is that these words and my experience with Father Gordon will encourage you to seek a spiritual director and to make that time together a priority. You and I need the help of these spiritual friends to be reminded again and again that we are beloved by God.

Father Gordon Moreland with Father Brad and Erik Karelius. May 2021.
Photo by Janice Karelius.

Chapter Nine

Meeting God at the Rose Bowl
Coach Tom Hamilton and Stacy Harvey

My father managed to pursue victory without the loss of his own
soul. He really did care deeply about winning. But that drive never
diminished his basic instinct to inspire and support those around
him.

—Tom Hamilton, Jr.[1]

Watching a football game, I'm offered a noble vision of life and challenges that echo the challenges that I face at work. The fight that's
going on in a football game, the strategy, that's real to me.

—Tom McGrath.[2]

Some people come into our lives, and we are never the same again. Their
presence, friendship, and honesty, especially at times of discernment, help
to shape who we were meant to be: our true selves.

I first met Coach Tom Hamilton in May 1960. I was soon to graduate
from Wilson Junior High School in Pasadena. A classmate and I sneaked
into the Pasadena High School varsity spring football practice at the old

1. Hamilton, Correspondence, September 6, 2021.
2. McDermatt, "Men are Struggling with their Spirituality," *America*, May 8, 2019.

Smokestack Field on the campus of Pasadena City College. There was no way that we were supposed to be there. Was it coincidence or God's amazing grace that I should be there on that day? We lined up for "non-contact" scrimmage. Before we started, varsity coach Dick Simmons announced in his bold voice, "I want you to meet our new varsity head football coach, Tom Hamilton."

And so it began.

In the first play of the practice scrimmage, Rick Flood, a pulling guard two years older than me, blasted through the line, crashed into me and busted my nose. Blood spurted everywhere. Coach Hamilton walked me over to the sidelines, told me to lie down and be still. The staff later escorted me off the field and admonished me to come back when I was actually a PHS student. Little did I know then that for forty-four years, Tom would become my best friend and mentor.

Coach Hamilton began a long, successful run as PHS football coach that Fall at the new Pasadena High School campus on Sierra Madre Boulevard. In tenth grade, all our home football games were in the Rose Bowl, because the Pasadena City College field was being renovated. The Rose Bowl. Imagine: high school athletes playing football at the the site of the Super Bowl, the National Collegiate Football championships, the Olympic Games and FIFA Women's World Cup Soccer! On the PHS team, I made lifelong friendships with teammates Bruce Corker, Pat Cayce, Gary Griffiths, Dennis Cosso, Rob Johnston, Stan Wood, and Greg Vartanian.

Coach Hamilton's first year of coaching in 1960 was a disaster. The varsity team lost every league game. Those first three years at the new PHS campus were a building time for the program, which finally culminated on November 1962 in the annual rivalry game between the two Pasadena schools, John Muir High and PHS at the venerable Rose Bowl. The intense rivalry drew thirty-five-thousand fans. Both schools celebrated Homecoming then, to draw out the loyal alumni. We had lost the game eight years in a row. But now with the score tied fourteen to fourteen, and seconds to go, quarterback Phil Olwin ran a broken play into the end zone for a touchdown. That victory was the high point of our senior year. The football team joyfully carried Coach Hamilton on their shoulders off the field. Coach Hamilton's career took off from there and carried him through the 1970s. His teams rarely lost a game and usually beat John Muir High School after that.

Coach Tom Hamilton with football team; victory over John Muir High School in the Rose Bowl, Pasadena, California, November, 1962. Pasadena Sports Hall of Fame.

With over four-thousand students in grades ten through twelve, PHS channeled hundreds of young men through sports programs. I was a face in the crowd, not the greatest athlete. Tom Hamilton coached me in football and baseball. Teenagers have special radar for hypocrisy and facades. I could see in Tom an honorable, good man. I think that was the spark that inspired further contact with him when I was in college and seminary.

Somewhere in the late 1960s, my teammate Gary Griffiths was on a U.S. Navy ship off the coast of Vietnam, studying football theory in his free time and writing to Tom to tell him he wanted to be a coach. After discharge from the service, Gary would return to PHS as an English teacher and assistant coach. He would become head football coach after Coach Hamilton retired. At about the same time, I wrote to Tom that I wanted to become a priest.

A lesson Tom gave all of us in athletics was this: there is a place deep within us, when we are beyond thirst, beyond tired, when we do not believe we can give any more, there is a place deep within us where we find the fire to do that which we did not think we could do. I believe Coach Tom helped us connect with the fire deep within us, the fire that is the awakening of our true selves.

His colleagues bear this out. Coach Gary Griffiths has this to say: "He was just the most unforgettable person I've ever met. The most principled. I think the thing that sticks most in my mind was his concept that you play by the rules to win. Everything was done in the right way. So many coaches were unscrupulous. He set an example for all of us coaches to follow."[3]

Arcadia High School football coach Dick Salter remembers his beloved friend. (Coach Salter told me that he played poker with Tom the week before the annual game between the two schools. The coach that won the poker game usually had the team that won the football game). "The coach I respected most was Tom Hamilton. He had such high integrity. More than anything else, he was a great person. He was a person of high character and great motivational skills for his kids. He ran wishbone for a while, he ran an unbalanced line like Michigan State, he ran the veer for a while, the 'I' formation. He would adjust to the personnel he had. When he had a good quarterback, he'd run the option. That's why Tom did so well. He utilized his people well. Even if you lost to him, you felt good, because he was such a good person."[4]

Former PHS football player Mickey Segal, President of the Rose Bowl Legacy Foundation, remembers: "Coach Hamilton was an inspiring leader. He was able to get 110% performance from every player. But more importantly, he was able to teach and develop character and responsibility in each and every one of us."[5]

After I graduated from seminary in 1970, I visited Tom at a football practice. He invited me to pray a blessing for the team the following week. From that day until the 1990s, I drove at least one-hundred-fifty miles almost every Friday night to be with Coach Tom and Coach Gary, as the chaplain to the PHS varsity team.

An image burns in my mind: we are in the Rose Bowl locker room, the most famous football stadium in America, for the annual Turkey Tussle football game against John Muir High School. Tom has helped the players focus again on that fire deep within. We kneel on the Astroturf carpet, in a

---

3. Hung, *Pasadena Star News*, March 15, 2004.

4. Hung, *Pasadena Star News*, March 15, 2004.

5. "Foundation to Dedicate," *Rose Bowl Stadium*, https://rosebowlstadium.com/news/23/dedication-tunnel-4.

compact circle, clasping heavily taped hands, the Muir High School drums beat a primal cadence that echoes within the bowels of the stadium and right outside our locker room door. I pray that God will keep all players safe from injury, that they will do their best and play a good, clean game. Has there been another day when we have felt more alive, felt more like brothers, and blessed to be with Coach Tom Hamilton?

Many are tempted to add success to success, onward and ever upward in an unthinking trajectory. But this was not the case with Coach Hamilton; none was more successful, but yet he stayed with the team.

In the wisdom of Celtic spirituality, we are adjured to remain planted where we are, to stay in place, to resist the allure of greener pastures. Spiritual writer Philip Sheldrake reflects:

> The desert tradition of monastic life, by which Celtic, especially Irish, spirituality may have been influenced, placed a central emphasis on the importance of staying in one place, specifically the cell, in order to find God.[6]

The commitment to be planted where you are is an invitation to the Holy Spirit to help you dig deep into the soil of your life and to attend to the needs of the world around you.

Tom had several opportunities to go for the "bigger and better": assistant coach at the University of Southern California; head coach and athletic director at Santa Monica High School—where he could focus completely on football; coach at an Orange County high school. Yet Tom decided again and again to remain where he was at PHS. Those decisions were hard, because the demands on coaching were soon to take a dramatic turn.

I frequently visited Tom at his home in Altadena which he shared with his life partner, Dr. Lynne Emory, a kinesiology professor at Cal Poly, Pomona, and acclaimed historian on women in the Olympic Games. I might find Tom in his garage working on carpentry. He built a fabulous dining room table, cribs for grandchildren and bookcases. Or I would find him working in the garden with Lynne. He would drop everything and take me into the living room of his modest home. Lynne made coffee and Tom had Royal Crown Cola. We talked. There was a presence to him. He was my best friend, and only after he died did I learn that many men like me felt ourselves to be his adopted sons.

---

6. Sheldrake, *Living Between Worlds*, 60.

Tom was "father-confessor" as I struggled with a decision to go to Maryland as rector of a large, well-to-do Episcopal church. He helped me focus on where my real passion was and still is: urban ministry in a struggling, multicultural, inner-city church in the Logan Barrio in Santa Ana. He helped me to remain in place, and from that decision, new ministries were birthed: an after-school tutoring and youth center to counter rising gang violence and an early childhood education center for the poorest families of Santa Ana.

Once when our son was in the hospital and his life hung by a thread, I received a surprise phone call from Rabbi Harold Kushner, author of *Why Bad Things Happen to Good People*. His own son had died ten years earlier. We talked about what it feels like being a religious professional, and how God can seem far away when we are in crisis ourselves and our loved ones are suffering. Then Rabbi Kushner quoted from his recent book:

> One of my favorite aphorisms comes from a nineteenth-century Hasidic rabbi who once said, 'Human beings are God's language.' When we call out to God in our distress, God answers us by sending us people.[7]

I do not believe God caused Erik's many health crises and suffering. God was with us in the people He sent: medical staff, therapists, and Coach Tom's many phone calls and personal visits. In the dark nights of my soul, Tom Hamilton has been God's language to me. He always accepted me as I was and where I was. If he did not hear from me for a while, he called me. He helped me to stay in touch with the fire that burns within and to resist the allures of the false self—who I am, what I do, what I have, what others think of me—and to focus on my true self, which has something to do with spending myself for the needs of others.

In the late 1970s, a shift in the demographics of the Pasadena Unified School system challenged Coach Tom Hamilton to adapt to a new cultural world. Coach Hamilton became "Coach Ham."

For decades, Pasadena had some of the best schools in California, influenced by their connection to the California Institute of Technology. When I attended PHS in the early 1960s, the quality of education was comparable to an excellent private school today. The student body was mostly white, with perhaps five percent African-American and five percent

---

7. Kushner, *Conquering Fear*, 171.

Asian-American. Some of my classmates were born in Manzanar and other World War II relocation camps.

My father attended John Muir Technical High School in the 1930s. The school covered the northwest sector of Pasadena which encompassed a vibrant Black community dating back to the 1880s. Jackie Robinson and his brother Mack were outstanding athletes at John Muir and were on the same sports teams as my father and his brothers, Earl and Kenneth. As I read Jackie Robinson's autobiography, I noticed only brief mention of his high school days. His experience of racism at the school and segregation at local recreational facilities affected his remembrance of those early days in Pasadena.

In 1970, a federal court ordered desegregation busing because of "de facto" segregation in the northwest sector of the district, which could affect equal access to quality education. White students dominated the other areas of the city. The Pasadena Unified School Board fought the court decision for a decade. Yet Pasadena High School became very multicultural and there was a significant white flight to schools in Arcadia, San Marino, and La Crescenta. Private schools had waiting lists and new private schools were launched.

The demographics of PHS and its sports teams changed to be more reflective of the real world. Tom became a multicultural coach. The classroom teaching and coaching roles changed. As mothers and fathers had to both work to support their families, teachers and coaches took on the roles of parents, helping with homework, health-care, and as personal advisors.

Tom Hamilton, Jr. remembers his father: "My father enjoyed helping people. He had a special gift of being a safe harbor, a person that people gravitated to when they were in trouble. His players, their parents, other P.H.S. students, fellow faculty and even administrators would seek him out to chat for a while. Later, they would leave, somehow calmer and more ready to face the trials of the world."[8]

Violent gang life encroached on Pasadena schools just as in the Logan Barrio, where my parish was in Santa Ana. The Bloods and Crips gangs preyed on vulnerable youth, offering alternative "family" and a downward life leading to prison, drug addiction or death. Sports teams and coaches like Tom Hamilton saved many young men, giving them vision and hope for the future.

How did Tom adjust to this cultural shift and establish rapport with the Black and Latino students? He was the same coach, the same mentor and teacher, who cared deeply about each player.

8. Hamilton, Correspondence, September 6, 2021.

One of these young men from the Black neighborhood of northwest Pasadena was Stacy Harvey. Stacy joined the team, as gang life tugged at him and his friends. He came to varsity football in the last years of Tom's coaching. Physically and charismatically larger than life, he was the quarterback and a natural leader. I have an indelible memory of Stacy in his last game against John Muir High School in 1982. The play was quarterback keeper. From the fifty yard line of the Rose Bowl, Stacy blasted through the middle of the line and, like a Sherman tank, continued straight up the field with two Muir players hanging on to him, as he carried them all the way to a touchdown.

**Stacy Harvey at Turkey Tussle football game, Rose Bowl, c. 2015.
Author's collection.**

When defense was on the field, I often sat with Stacy on the bench and our friendship grew. I stayed in touch with him as he went off to Arizona State University. He had an outstanding four years playing football, culminating in his team's victory over Michigan in the Rose Bowl. As a linebacker, Stacy led the team with eleven tackles in that game.

He had a long career in management with Los Angeles County Public Works, raised a family, and stayed connected to his PHS friends in the northwest Pasadena neighborhood. Our friendship became closer during the five years we worked together on the Board of the PHS Alumni Association. The school has a history going back to the 1880s, with thousands of alumni, but Stacy and his classmates of 1983 were the only ones to launch an alumni association. The Alumni Board met every month. Around the table were the men and women who grew up with Stacy in his neighborhood. All the men had played football and remembered me as a priest to the team. I am grateful to have been drawn into the lives of these men and women and to see their devotion to their families, their church, their careers and especially to PHS. As President, Stacy had a forceful presence and he could motivate us to donate scholarships, organize campus work projects and fund equipment for athletic programs.

Stacy had a big heart spiritually, but his physical heart grew weak. I visited Stacy at Huntington Hospital after his heart bypass surgery. This health crises had also been a spiritual catharsis. He knew that he had almost died and intended to make amends with friends and family. God was close to him. A few weeks later, Stacy died in his sleep.

Powerful expressions of love and appreciation for Stacy filled the Pasadena High School auditorium at his memorial service. Twenty of his teammates from Arizona State University attended, as well as dozens of rival John Muir High School football alums. Stacy's son spoke about his father—not only his sports legacy but also as a beloved family man.

Ironically, a few weeks before he died, Stacy had planned a picnic at Brookside Park to thank all the people who helped him during his illness. The afternoon of that planned picnic was the day of his memorial service. Lifelong friends from the northwest Pasadena neighborhood, a devoted extended family, celebrated the reunion that Stacy had planned.

Coach Tom Hamilton's life was cut short by lung cancer. Tom did not smoke, but asbestos at the PHS facility could have caused the disease. Up to then, he seemed to always be in training, walking several miles early each morning around the Rose Bowl with his beloved Lynne Emery. The cancer drained him. He struggled for each breath. I have this memory: I am with Tom at his home. A bleak winter day. I help administer morphine under his tongue to assuage the panic that comes with a dying lung. I hold his big hand and gaze out the window at a bird on a barren tree branch. I feel helpless. As a priest, I have been with many parishioners who were dying, but this was different. There are no words to say, all I can do is hold on tight and channel my love for him. Coach Gary Griffiths was a caregiver for Tom in those last days. Two days after my visit, Gary called me to say that our beloved Tom had died.

October 31, 2019, I am again at the Rose Bowl. This time I am with former coaches and players to dedicate Tunnel Four in memory of Coach Tom Hamilton. It was a few hours before the annual John Muir High School–PHS rivalry football game. Coach Hamilton's son, Tom Hamilton, Jr, and his family welcomed the gathering. Then Tom flipped the coin at the traditional coin toss before the game began.

Here is a little of what I said at that dedication: "Tom is imbedded in this Rose Bowl. He played in the first Turkey Tussle game in 1947. Most of the home games of his early coaching years were right here in the Rose Bowl. When he retired, he walked around the stadium every morning at 6:30 with his beloved Dr. Lynne Emery.

"I believe the last time Tom came to the Pasadena-Muir game at the Rose Bowl, he entered with me through this Tunnel Four. As we walked through the tunnel down the long steps to the grassy playing field to be with the team, it took at least a half hour, because the aisle was filled with former players, now fathers and grandfathers, and police officers, who wanted to greet again their beloved coach."[9]

In a reversal of the image of the stairway to heaven, I imagine this: Coach Tom Hamilton and Stacy Harvey walking down the stairs of the Rose Bowl, slowly passing by former players and coaches, friends and fans, and teammates, as they walk arm in arm onto the field of glory.

Lord God, as I wrote this reflection on Tom and Stacy, you awakened in me again my love for these two good men, my friends, and my grief still aches. Thank you, surprising and generous God, for inviting me into their lives, for the genuine gift of deep, honest, joyful friendship with them. Rest eternal grant to them and may light perpetual shine upon them. Amen.

9. Karelius, *Dedication of Tunnel Four*, October 31, 2019.

Chapter Ten

Aztec Poet and Teacher

David Vazquez

IT IS A WARM Good Friday evening. At the corner of Main Street and Civic Center Drive in Santa Ana, David Vazquez is carrying a heavy ten-foot cross on his shoulder. He made it himself by lashing two logs together with rope. Luis Lopez helps keep it steady. We are at the head of a procession of about two hundred people. I am standing next to David on the curb as we wait for the police to stop the traffic so that we can cross Main. I look at his solemn brown face, his prominent, noble nose and the rope of a plait that goes all the way down to his waist. He has the shoulders of a man who is accustomed to hard physical work. Outward Aztec warrior strength belies spiritual depth.

We wind our way along the sidewalks of downtown for three miles, stopping at certain points: there are fourteen stations of the cross. At each someone holds upright the cross and, alternating English and Spanish, various readers proclaim the gospel above the city bustle, recalling Jesus' journey to his crucifixion at Golgotha, the Place of the Skull, a hill outside Jerusalem. Then the reader offers a prayer from the heart and the procession continues with the pilgrims singing traditional hymns: *Perdona Tu Pueblo, Señor* —Forgive Your People, Dear Lord, and *Amazing Grace*. Men, women and teenagers take turns at carrying the cross.

The stations are all places that could use our prayers: a university health clinic, an encampment of homeless people, a job-training workshop for low-income youth. At the Orange County Jail, a mother stands on a low wall next to the cross to read the scripture and to pray for the prisoners, her own son among them.

If this were happening in Laguna Beach, Irvine or Fullerton, observers would wonder what was going on, but here in the city with the highest proportion of native Spanish-speakers in the United States, our public Good Friday observance is not at all foreign. Santa Ana has grown to embrace people from every Latin American country. They remember the solemn *Via Crucis* processions back home; men remove their hats, women kneel on the concrete, and the line of pilgrims becomes longer and longer

My thoughts turn to David again. He is a remarkable man. He has changed my life—made all our lives better. I think about how our paths converged as I (of Swedish forebears!) found myself nurturing a burgeoning Latino congregation; and as he grew into being a teacher, poet and artist and revived an ancient language.

When I arrived as the new pastor at Messiah parish in 1981, the remnants of the area's pioneer Anglo-families were struggling to keep the doors open. The church had once thrived as the parish of the Irvine and Moulton ranching families and the owners of the Orange County Register, among many other luminaries. But as Latino immigrants began settling here in the 1970s, the old guard had retreated to South County or to northern California. Walking the neighborhood, I would hear Spanish rather than English. A giant apartment block had been built two streets away, and another, and another . . . sometimes three families to each apartment. Underfunded, crowded schools, gang violence, people working too hard, despair. . . . If Messiah was to be a church for this barrio, then I would have to change. After eleven years as a priest in affluent Laguna Beach I was a fish out of water, a cleric misplaced.

A gifted teacher, Raquel Salcines, who had been among the dozen Cuban-refugee families sponsored by Messiah parish in the 1960s, gave me intensive Spanish lessons. I put up a banner on the side of the Church: *Misa en Español Domingo al Mediodia. Todos Bienvenidos,* (Mass in Spanish, Sunday Noon. All Welcome). The first people to attend were the Cuban-Americans.

A week later, the assisting priest at St. Joseph's Roman Catholic Church visited me. He said that the banner was misleading Latinos into thinking we were a Catholic church, Misa being a Catholic term. I responded: "We are a Catholic church. Anglican Catholic. We believe in the Real Presence of Jesus in the Sacrament, just as you do. But I assure you, if I think someone is looking for a Roman church, I will send them to you." That was in 1983. As time passed, I developed strong personal ties with the pastors at St. Joseph's.

Attendance at the Spanish Mass increased. The families in the neighborhood found it to be similar to that of their Roman Catholic roots. They were pleased to see a priest who was married. Not only that, but by then we also had a woman priest serving the congregation, and people liked that too. We built relationships over long coffee hours after the Misa and a number of well-received programs began as a result. For instance, an immigration attorney was called in to help with documentation problems—something that almost all the Latino families had to deal with.

Then one Sunday in 1989, David Vazquez appeared with his guitar and joined our Russian-Brazilian pianist in accompanying the music for the Misa. And I and the parish were never the same again.

David and I went out for coffee. He had just arrived from Mexico where he had been a construction worker in Mexico City. His home had been in a poor and isolated village of two-hundred people in the state of Puebla. As a boy, he had foraged for mushrooms in the woods to exchange for the essentials for his family.

He soon became a faithful member of our music team and when we needed to hire a new custodian for the parish, I knew he was the man for the job. Through the offices of the Episcopal Diocese of Los Angeles we secured the immigration papers for David as a church worker. Now he had a regular salary, health insurance, and a pension plan. Before long, his wife, Rosa, arrived with their children, and they were able to put down roots in what had become a vibrant immigrant parish.

The church building itself is a vulnerable Victorian wooden construction. David became its guardian angel. He would begin work at six in the morning. Perhaps a storm during the night meant that the sump pumps in the basement needed fixing and the roof had to be inspected for leaks. Perhaps he had to clean up after another break-in. Morning Garden, the early-childhood program for homeless mothers and children, began at eight. In the afternoon seventy-five raucous teenagers would descend on the Noah Project Youth Center in the basement. In the evenings, the sanctuary might be filled with parents and friends for a performance by the Orange County High School of the Arts. Wednesday afternoons meant that the basement kitchen would be busy with the preparation of a street-meal for two-hundred homeless people at the Civic Center. All of this and more meant an endless round of setting-up and fixing and finding and cleaning. David did it all and Rosa would help.

I have a limited knowledge of Mexican life, but I was astonished to discover that David had not learned Spanish until he was thirteen. The language of his village is the ancient Nahuatl of the Aztecs. In fact, almost two-million Mexicans speak Nahuatl as their first language. For many years David had been nurturing a desire to teach his mother-tongue which, suppressed during centuries of Spanish occupation, had become an underground, strictly oral language, its written form lost. He developed an Aztec alphabet.

For National Public Radio, Lori Galarretta had this to say:

> One day as a young boy in Tlalmotolo, he wrote random symbols on maguey-plant leaves, putting them in no particular order at first, not knowing what he was doing. He didn't think of them as letters until he found out later that Nahuatl's original writing system didn't survive the Conquest. Once he completed the alphabet in 1968, he practiced writing it so he could memorize the new system before sharing it with Tlalmotolo's elders; they approved.[1]

In 1996, David got permission to offer free Nahuatl language classes on Saturdays in the parish choir room, and for over twenty years these classes continued at Messiah, branching out to community centers in the area and to the universities, UCLA and Cal-State Northridge. Jose Vega shares his enthusiasm for David's work: "I've been coming to these classes for close to four months now. I just had to get a better understanding of what the past was. Now we're living, and we don't know who we are or where we came from. Some of us don't bother to look back and see who our people used to be or the way they used to live."[2]

What drove David to invest so much of himself into developing this half-forgotten language? This is what he had to say: "My story is a difficult tale, but something pushes me, obligates me to be a leader. On the one hand, I like it, and on the other hand, perhaps the Divine worked through me to create something sacred, and that is the Nahuatl writing system."[3]

1. Galarreta, "One Man's Mission."
2. Galarreta, "One Man's Mission."
3. Galarreta, "One Man's Mission."

David connected to the fire and passion within him, his spirituality, and it sustained him in pursuing a project that has inspired thousands of students.

On a blustery December morning, the parishioners gather in the dim dawn for the misa of Our Lady of Guadalupe. In this we celebrate the appearance in 1531 of the Virgin Mary to a poor farmer, Juan Diego, on the Hill of Tepeyac, outside Mexico City. In several appearances to Juan Diego, the dark-skinned Virgin spoke Nahuatl. After the gospel-reading, David comes to the lectern to recite, in Nahuatl, a poem of praise and gratitude for Our Lady of Guadalupe. I close my eyes and I can hear David's voice now, the soft, liquid flow of a beautiful language I do not know—a spirit voice.

Hundreds of people for whom Nahuatl was their first language had settled in Santa Ana over the years. The Superior Court (a few blocks from Messiah) needed interpreters of Nahuatl and other indigenous languages. With the help of one of his students, Lupe Lopez, and after rigorous testing, David got the job. This, of course, was important work: helping people who would otherwise have little access to justice, and I do not diminish it, but I think of him mostly as a significant churchman—a leader of a parish that was hard at work to remake itself.

In the afternoon of the third Sunday of December, parents and parishioners fill the church in anticipation of the *Presentacion de Nacimiento,* the Christmas pageant played by the children. A ten-year-old girl in a blue costume sits on a wooden donkey which is led by Joseph up the aisle to the altar as the people sing a carol. Then the angels and shepherds and kings join in the reenactment of the birth of Jesus. Such tableaux are quite usual all over the Christian world at this time of year, but the Latinos are just getting started. David now leads the *Posada* procession in which Mary and Joseph and the donkey and the choir of angels and the whole assembly throng excitedly through the sedate Victorian-era neighborhood of French Park. David has selected in advance four homes to visit. At each I play the innkeeper and I stand behind the bolted front-door while Mary and Joseph and the parishioners sing the traditional doleful verses, pleading for *posada*—shelter for the night. The innkeeper and the people of the house sing out their verses, telling the vagabonds to go away. At each home that we visit there is a *nacimiento,* a nativity scene, which I bless with holy water.

So, we make our way to the next inn and the next one, all the way we sing the traditional carols of Latin America. By the time we are ready to turn back to the church, the night has become cold and windy. It is a long way but nobody falters, David leading as ever. At the church again, the doors are locked against Mary and Joseph and the people. And again they knock on the door and sing out the three verses. Now is the time for the fourth verse. I always love hearing its touching style:

> My wife is Mary
> She is the Queen of Heaven
> and she is going to be the mother
> of the Divine Word.
> This time, the innkeeper responds:
> Are you Joseph?
> Your wife is Mary?
> Enter, pilgrims;
> I did not recognize you.

The church doors burst open. Come on in! The music changes to a joyful cadence as the crowd presses into the parish hall.

Beginning early in the morning, David and his wife and some other resolute parishioners have been making a thousand tamales, chicken, pork and sweet, along with champurrado and *punche*. The fine, rustic fare warms body and soul. Soon the patio is filled with over-active children, eager for the piñata-bashing to begin. I hold my breath as the blindfolded girls and boys wave the stick wildly, trying to whack the piñata into releasing its bounty of candy.

David inspired and organized many such parish celebrations that were to bridge the gap between the Anglo and Latino cultures. In October we would celebrate Hispanic Heritage Month with a special bilingual Mass, followed by a lunch of dishes from all over Latin America. On the Sunday closest to November first, the Misa of All Saints began on the church patio where an *ofrenda* altar had been built in the middle. So we also marked the *Dia de los Muertos,* the Day of the Dead (All Souls Day). The altar would be decorated with photographs and mementos of the recently-deceased loved ones of the parish. And around the altar too would be the *pan del muertos* (bread of the dead), marigolds, and skulls of colored sugar and ceramic. I can see David now as he paces reverently around the altar with an Aztec-inspired censer filled with burning incense. Thus, the Christian liturgy of All Saints Day and the indigenous Day of the Dead traditions merged on our church patio.

David developed serious health issues in 2020 and in February 2021 his vulnerable body succumbed to COVID–19.

In 1989, an undocumented stranger from the remote village of Tlal-motolo arrived to play his guitar at the Misa of an Episcopal church in Santa Ana. The parish was never the same after that. We were all touched and inspired by this gifted musician, poet and artist.

David Vazquez at Messiah Parish, Santa Ana, California, 2017. Author's collection.

Chapter Eleven

Ways of Prayer for Men
Liturgy of the Hours

We must know that God regards our purity of heart and tears of compunction, not our many words. Prayer should therefore be short and pure, unless perhaps it is prolonged under the inspiration of divine grace. In Community, however, prayer should always be brief, and when the superior gives the signal, all should rise together.

—ESTHER DE WAAL[1]

I HAVE BEEN A parish priest for fifty years, but this is no qualification for faithful prayer. It has been a distracted, multitasking career in which I have not been faithful to the haunting, persistent pull of God's desire for communion with me.

After two different bouts with cancer and several decades of care for our disabled son, Erik, the patient caresses of the Spirit have worn down my resistant distraction, turning my face toward God in prayer.

Father Ron Rolheiser, in his book *Holy Longing* describes the challenging situation you and I face as we consider prayer practices that nourish men. He writes:

1. De Waal, *Life Giving Way*, 86.

Inside of us, it would seem, something is at odds with the very rhythm of things, and we are forever restless, dissatisfied, frustrated and aching. We are so overcharged with desire that it is hard to come to simple rest.

We are driven persons, forever obsessing, congenitally diseased, living lives of quiet desperation, only occasionally experiencing peace. Desire is the straw that stirs the drink.

Spirituality is about what we do with that desire. What we do with our longings. Augustine said: "You have made us for yourself, Lord, and our hearts are restless until they rest in you." Spirituality is about what we do with our unrest.[2]

Our innate holy longing is for experiences of communion and connection with the Lord Jesus. Are these words speaking to you? I believe you are reading this book because you recognize your deepest longing is to be in communion with God in our Lord Jesus Christ. My desire for you is that you will find some practical assistance for your prayer life to nurture your Holy Longing for the Lord.

What forms of prayer might be especially suitable for men? Here is an approach we will take to answer this question, as suggested by Father Ron Rolheiser, OMI:

Prayer has the power to transform our inner spirit and how we experience God in the movement of everyday life. Sustaining a daily life of prayer that does not demand of us energy we cannot muster, includes familiar and repetitious ritual that is clearly defined and time limited.[3]

With this in mind, in the following chapters I present three forms of structured prayer to foster a discipline of daily prayer.

First, the Daily Office of the breviary—the Liturgy of the Hours, as a way of praying throughout the day and reflecting upon the Word of God.

Second, the Examen of consciousness: a daily practice of gratitude and discernment of God's movements in our life.

Third, centering prayer or contemplative prayer: practicing the presence of God and listening for God's inspiration as to how we might live our lives.

2. Rolheiser, *Holy Longing*, 6–7.

3. Rolheiser, "Sustaining A Prayer Life," https://ronrolheiser.com/sustaining-a-prayer-life/#.YJwu4KhKjE4.

Spiritual writer Henri Nouwen said that the essential thing about prayer is you must show up for prayer regularly. Sometimes my heart is deeply moved by a sense of God's embrace; much of the time I am bored, distracted and looking at the clock: how much time before my twenty minutes is up? But I stay with my scheduled prayer, mostly. Here is an analogy that has helped me. When my father was ninety-eight, he lived in a board-and-care home a few blocks from our own home in Laguna Niguel, California. Of his three children, I was the only one who lived close by. I faithfully visited day after day, around noon. I helped him with his lunch. We talked about the news and golf games. He could precisely remember PGA golf scores from the day before. After lunch, we would go back to his room and our trivial banter continued—nothing too serious. Occasionally, he would tell me a story about his work adventures in South America. I would find myself glancing at the clock to see when I might gracefully depart. These daily visits continued over months and months. I had the privilege of getting to know my father more deeply, and he got to know me more deeply. At a certain level of our relationship, the actual connection between us took place below the surface of our conversation. We came to know each other through simple presence.

Prayer is like this: praying faithfully every day, through weeks, months, years, bored, looking at the clock. But under the surface between you and me and God, a deeper bond is growing.

We have passed through the first stages of the COVID-19 pandemic, when most of us were at home, in our monastic cells, if you will, minimizing social contact. How can Christian monks help us to grow our life with God? I have found that a detailed schedule for the day has given me a sense of order, sanity, and control as I try to avoid latching on to this or that distraction, junk-food or ephemeral entertainment. Finding a prayer practice is part of this order. Some days I pray the Examen, some days I concentrate on contemplative prayer or the Liturgy of the Hours.

One of the gifts to us from monastic culture is the Liturgy of the Hours, that is, the breviary and the Daily Office. These canonical hours were influenced by the Jewish schedule of daily prayers. Early Christians adapted this practice when they moved into the deserts of Syria, Palestine, and Egypt. They became whom we know as the desert fathers and mothers, establishing the first Christian monastic communities.

Monasticism flourished for a while, but then discipline broke down, coincidental with the division of the Roman Empire, and conflict inside the monasteries became common. Saint Benedict lived in these turbulent times and in response developed in AD 516 *The Rule* which became a guidebook for sustaining Christian religious communities. 1500 years later it is still very much in use.

The Rule gives guidance as to how to live a Christocentric life on Earth and how to administer a monastery efficiently. Benedict's golden rule was *Ora et Labora*, pray and work, or put another way, *Orare est Laborare*, to pray is to work, to work is to pray: a structured schedule of prayer for eight hours, sleep for eight hours, and manual labor or sacred reading for eight hours.

Benedict gives us direction as we ponder what prayer forms are best suited to us. In his plan for scheduled prayer, we do not have to come up with our own words to pray. The dominant use of the psalms brings men in touch with their feelings and emotions percolating within—men in particular benefit from this. The prayer services all can be said in ten to fifteen minutes.

Chapters 8–10 of the Rule regulate the Divine Office with eight canonical hours, fixed times for prayer. Here is the original schedule proposed by Benedict. The *horarium* began at midnight with Matins. This was followed by Lauds at 3AM (before wax candles came into use in the fourteenth century, the monks had to memorize the service in order to pray in the dark). Then, every three hours throughout the day there would be a designated time for prayer; Prime, Terce, Sext, None, Vespers, and Compline or Night Prayer at 9PM.

Several variations of the schedule have developed over time. After the Second Vatican Council in the 1960s, a new arrangement of the Liturgy of the Hours was encouraged. The Anglican Church radically simplified Benedict's prayer schedule in the *Book of Common Prayer*, combining the first three services into Matins/Morning Prayer and the latter two into Vespers/Evening Prayer. However, Anglican religious and monastic communities retained the eight original prayer services of Benedict.

I remember forty years of retreats at the Anglican-Episcopal monastery of Mount Calvary of the Order of the Holy Cross, in an old Spanish-style hacienda, in the mountains above Montecito, with views up and down the California coast. A brass bell rings outside at 5:45AM in the cold darkness of December. I jolt up from the bed in my cell, pull on a thick hooded sweatshirt and jeans, and shuffle down the hall over the creaky wooden floor towards the chapel. Dawn is breaking in the distance as I gaze through the large chapel window, observing the twinkling street lights of Ventura to the south. I find a seat in a long pew on one side of the altar behind the monks, who seem to have their own personal seats.

We stand as the Prior enters and Prime begins. We sit for the chanting of several long psalms. The words are printed in a special breviary with pointed marks where the tone changes and there is a dot at the end of the first half of each sentence. In this way, one side of the chapel chants the first part of the sentence and the other side knows when to respond antiphonally. Praying these long psalms, I would take a deep breath to chant my part and found that everyone on my side of the chapel eventually synchronized their breathing. There was a hypnotic rhythm to the chanting and the breathing. These monks have been chanting and praying the Liturgy of the Hours for decades. Each of the eight prayer services spread out over the day takes ten to fifteen minutes.

I made several retreats to Mount Calvary Monastery during low points of Erik's health. During those times I felt numb and my muscles ached all the time with internalized stress. I had great difficulty reading or chanting the prayer services, but the communal voice of the monks lifted me up as I struggled to participate.

> Sustaining a life of prayer that does not demand of us energy we cannot muster, it includes familiar and repetitious ritual that is clearly defined and time limited.[4]

Roman Catholic priests and deacons pray all the hours of the breviary. The laity are encouraged to pray Lauds (Morning Prayer) and Vespers (Evening Prayer). The Church of England and Episcopal Church *Book of Common Prayer* also have these daily liturgical prayers, all coming out of the Benedictine monastic tradition. Some Lutheran traditions use the *Brotherhood Prayer Book*.

When I first tried to pray the Liturgy of the Hours in my leather-bound copy of the breviary, I was confused as to where the lessons and canticles were to be found. You have to flip back and forth between sections in order to get it right. Using the breviary can be intimidating at first, but if you follow the system step-by-step you will find that it will work for you.

I use the *Christian Prayer* edition. You will see several colored ribbons which are very important to help you find the parts of each prayer service.

---

4. Rolheiser, "Sustaining a Prayer Life," https://ronrolheiser.com/sustaining-a-prayer-life/#.YkZdzSjMLE4.

If you have this edition, start on page six hundred and eighty-six. This is the Ordinary, a reference point you can always come back to when you pray the Liturgy of the Hours. The phrase "Say the black, do the red" means that all the red words printed on this page are instructions and all the black printed words are prayers that you pray. Read this whole page carefully before you continue.

Place the first ribbon where it says Invitatory. An antiphon and Psalm 95 are prayed before Morning Prayer. While the antiphons are printed only once, you recite the antiphon both before and after a psalm.

The second ribbon is placed in a section beginning on page 41. This section is called the Proper of Seasons. The Church seasons are Advent, Christmas, Epiphany, Lent, Easter, and Ordinary Time.

Catholic spiritual writer Philip Kosloski offers an excellent resource, *A Beginner's Guide to Praying the Liturgy of the Hours.* He shares this example as practice:

> Place the ribbon on page 344, "Fourth Week of Lent" and "Monday, Morning Prayer". To figure out the week, go to USCCB.org and click on calendar. Alternately, you can order your own wall liturgical calendar that says what day it is. When you reach the next Sunday, it says what Psalter you are currently in. It reads Psalter, Week IV below Fourth Sunday of Lent. This is where you put your third ribbon.
>
> This example exercise leads us to page 937, Monday, Week IV. If you get confused on which Psalter, go back to the Proper of the Seasons and the correct Sunday will tell you.
>
> The fourth ribbon marks the current day for Night Prayer. This is only a single cycle that repeats each week. For our example exercise this is on page 1041.
>
> The fifth ribbon marks the Proper of the Saints, with special prayers and antiphons for specific saints' days. You only need to know the calendar date to know the saint's day and where to put the ribbon. For our example, today is March 7, the Memorial of Perpetua and Felicity.[5]

As you get into the rhythm of daily prayer you will develop familiarity with the way it is done. Philip Kosloski encourages us:

> Praying in this manner, while more difficult than opening up an app, is very beneficial. In an age where everything is available at

---

5. Kosloski, "Beginner's Guide to Praying the Liturgy of the Hours," http://www.philipkosloski.com/a-beginners-guide-to-praying-the-liturgy-of-the-hours/.

the touch of your finger, it is healthy to learn the 'art' of praying the divine office.[6]

Having said the above, there is no doubt that it is complicated to find your way through all those ribbons. Thank God for my iPhone, where I found two helpful apps: I-breviary and Universalis. When I want to pray one of these hours, Compline, say, I click it and the whole service appears with the Psalms and lessons for the day. There is even an extra embellishment that allows a voice to lead you in the prayers. Another setting chants the entire liturgy of Compline in Latin.

Father Ron Rolheiser, OMI, shares this helpful understanding:

> We are no longer just a private individual praying: we are the voice, body and soul of the earth itself, continuing the high priesthood of Christ, offering prayers and entreaties, aloud and in silent tears, to go to do for the sake of the World.[7]

We can imagine Earth slowly spinning on its axis, turning from day into night, into day into night. If someone in Denver, Colorado prays the Vespers tonight at 9PM, an hour later the ball passes to me in California: the world turns on these continuous prayers of the people of God.

I find solace and connection with God every night in praying Compline. I usually pray it in the darkness of our bedroom. In this time you can take stock of your concerns about friends, family, work, finances, health, the future—and God's world. I like to make Compline my last activity before going to bed.

If you have trouble quieting your mind before sleep, perhaps after a disturbing or troubling day, this is the prayer setting for you. Some of the psalms appointed for the evening sound like they are coming from a dark, desperate place, others sing out joyfully in thanksgiving. As you get into the habit of praying them, you will find that they become your own voice to God. Often there is a mention of plague, disease, serious illness, calamity, troubles. The Psalms reflect the variety of human moods and emotions. They help you get in touch right now with what is moving within your own heart as you pray with God. The prayers invoke God's embrace of benevolent, protective love, enshrouding you and all those you love as you sleep into the night.

---

6. Kosloski, *Beginner's Guide to Praying the Liturgy of the Hours.*

7. Rolheiser, *Prayer,* 29.

This sounds inviting, but I find it hard to bring up the energy to pray all the Hours every day. You do not have to pray all the Hours. You can always bundle a few together to try them out, as you also consider the Examen of Conscience and contemplative prayer, which we will explore in the next chapters.

At lunch time, for instance, sitting outside in a garden, you may want to click the app for Afternoon Prayer. If you pray Compline, as I do every night, and you fall asleep in the middle of prayer, you are okay resting in God. The choices can change. The important thing is to *show up* for prayer friendship with God.

Remember, you are not praying alone. You join the voice of the Church, which is praying continuously around the world.

Sister Joan Chittister, OSB, shares:

> We go to prayer to be transfigured ourselves, to come to see the world as God sees the world, to practice the presence of God, to put on a heart of justice, of love, and of compassion for others.[8]

Most Monday evenings, I visit the home of a local Roman Catholic priest, joining two other Catholic clergy and another Episcopal priest, to pray Evening Prayer from the breviary. Dinner and animated conversations follow. We end the evening singing *Salve Regina,* a centuries-old song to Mary. Common prayers bridge historic ecclesiastical differences. Wine and good food warm hearts and nurture deep friendship. The Lord has told me he is very pleased.

So, reflect now—what are you asking from God today? And what did you find in this chapter that gives you hope for a more intentional schedule of prayer?

8. Chittister, *Called to Question,* 46.

Chapter Twelve

Ways of Prayer for Men
Examen of Conscience

WHEN I WAS FIVE years old, I attended Sunday School at the First Baptist Church on Washington Boulevard in Altadena, California. I remember informing my mother one day that I thought that my teacher, a woman, must be Jesus. Why? Because she embodied the love, compassion, and presence that I experienced in Jesus when she read the Bible stories to us.

Our teacher, Mrs. Heaton (I could never forget her name), asked us to close our eyes and imagine with our senses all that was going on when she read the Bible stories to us. Many of these stories were the classics about the patriarchs and prophets. At one point, after a story about Moses complaining to God in the Exodus wilderness, my eyes suddenly opened, and I blurted out: "How come Moses always forgot what God has already done for him? Didn't God help him find water and manna in the desert? Why does he always forget?"

Today, we can imagine someone complaining to a friend who had been helpful in the past: "Yes, but what have you done for me lately?"

Forgetfulness about all that God had already accomplished was a chronic spiritual problem for the prophets and patriarchs and I believe that forgetfulness is a spiritual problem for many, if not all of us.

The challenge is "to remember," from the Hebrew word *zakhor.* Zakhor appears two hundred times in the Hebrew Bible: remember the Sabbath, remember the Covenant, remember the Exodus from Egypt.

Zakhor, remembering, is crystalized in the Jewish Passover meal, the Seder. This is a sacred meal that involves all the human senses: the taste, touch, and smell of the Seder foods, symbolizing the Exodus experience; hearing and singing the joyful songs; and reading the sacred story from ages past when God liberated the Hebrew people from slavery. At some point in the Haggadah, the narrative booklet used to celebrate the Seder, the verb tenses change from past to present or the subjunctive: "In each generation, every person should see himself as if he personally came out of Egypt."[1] Zakhor brings the past into the present and forward into the future.

In the Sabbath and all their sacred holidays, the Jewish people are involved in a performance of memory through deeds, actions, and speech in the process of *not forgetting.*

In his classic book, *The Gifts of the Jews,* Thomas Cahill contends that it is the Jewish people who gave to the modern world the concepts of progress and future hope. The classical world was a world of repetitive cycles where nothing changed. In the Jewish experience of their sacred history, history is linear, leading forward to fulfillment of God's promises.

In all the pogroms and violence that the Jews have suffered in their long history as a people, how in the world could they sustain hope? Liturgically and sacramentally, they remembered with gratitude what God had already done. Thus, they could look to the future, as bleak as it may have appeared at the time, with faith in God's grace.

Zakhor has important meaning for Christians too. As the Passover Seder was a precursor to the Lord's Supper, Eucharist, Holy Communion, the belief in the real presence of Jesus in the bread and wine of the Eucharist is rooted in the Jewish idea of Zakhor. The Eucharist is not simply a memorial to an event long ago; it means that even today, now, in the breaking of the bread, Jesus is fully present with us and we are fully present with him. We remember:

Christ has died.

Christ is risen.

Christ will come again.

---

1. Rabbi Sachs, "Sense of History," https://rabbisacks.org/ki-tavo-a-sense-of-history/.

Five hundred years ago, a Spanish mystic, Ignatius Loyola, developed a prayer form that today, if followed faithfully, can give you and me a deeper awareness that the Lord Jesus is our companion. It can give a deeper sense of the remembering which leads to gratitude and awe at God's generous goodness.

The Examination of Consciousness, which Ignatius developed from his own prayer experience, can seem like a simple prayer format with five action points, but as you pray it, the prayer grows in complexity. This prayer can spark and awaken profound and important life-changing events that will call out gratitude to God.

The *Examen* reveals a map with marker points: not leading forward so much as looking back on your life, those crossroads, those grace-filled moments, when you were at the end of your resources—in a corner, in grief or panic—and it was then that God's grace broke through. Mapping those marker points of your own sacred history can show you that you have not been alone in your life. The Lord has been beside you all the way. And you realize that you can only be grateful for God working when you are in deep distress.

Gratitude is foundational to hope.

Hope without gratitude is wishful thinking.

I read in *Forbes* that we men generally define our self-worth by what others think of us, by what we *do*, how much money we have, what we have achieved and how we look. Multi-tasking can lead us in many distracting directions and away from our best self and our connection with God.[2]

To live more consciously in the presence of God, Ignatius gave us the Examen Prayer. In this brief, five-part prayer we spend a few moments reviewing our day, paying attention to when we felt God present with us and times when we felt separated from God. The prayer helps us live in gratitude for those people, situations, and events in our day when we are most grateful. The Examen reminds us of God's forgiveness.

I invite you to pray this Examen prayer with me. I pray this prayer every night before I go to sleep. Here is a description of the steps, with thanks to Father James Martin, SJ.[3]

1. Prepare: I invite God to be with me now as I pray. In gratitude. I recall two or three good things that happened today. I look back on any

---

2. "How Do You Measure Your Self-Worth," *Forbes*, January 18, 2015.

3. Martin, *Jesuit Guide to (Almost) Everything*, 95–100.

good news, precious moments, perhaps an encounter in nature. I focus on thanking God. A caution: do not rush through this. Savor and relish this revisiting of events for which you are grateful.

2. Ask for the grace to know your sins. As I look back on this day, where did I turn away from my true self, the deepest part of myself? Where did some curt remark or rudeness happen? Listen to your conscience and that deep voice leading you to be more loving. Do not beat up on yourself, but own your need for God's grace.

3. Anthony de Mello said, "Be grateful for your sins. They are carriers of grace."[4]

4. Review your day. This is the heart of the prayer. I imagine a video camera playing back my day, from when I first got up. I want to pay attention to where there was joy, confusion, conflict and moments of peace and love. Again, do not rush through this.

5. Forgiveness. Ask God for forgiveness for anything sinful done during the day. Look for the opportunity to make amends.

6. Ask for God's help tomorrow. Close with a prayer.

As with the Liturgy of the Hours, the Examen is another structured prayer that only takes fifteen minutes but can become transformative in your life with God. Remind yourself as you pray the Examen: this is not a dialogue with yourself; you are doing this reflection of the past day with God as present with you.

The Examen prayer helps us to see the presence of God as we look back on our life.

Father Peter Hans Kolvenback, SJ, tells this story about looking back to encounter God:

> There was an abbot in the Middle Ages who would speak to his monks every day "On finding God, on searching for God, on encountering God." One day a monk asked the abbot if he had ever encountered God? Had he ever had a vision or seen God face-to-face? After a long silence, the abbot answered frankly: No, he had not. "But", said the abbot, "there was not anything surprising in this because even to Moses in the Book of Exodus God said, 'You cannot see my face; for no one shall see me and live.' God says that Moses will see his back as he passed by him.

---

4. de Mello, *Wellsprings*, 227.

Thus, looking back over the length and breadth of his life the abbot could see for himself the passage of God.

In this sense, it is less a matter of searching for God than of allowing oneself to be found by Him in all of life's situations, where He does not cease to pass and where He allows Himself to be recognized once He has really passed.[5]

Here is a testimony of how the Examen prayer has helped a student at Marquette University:

> For me, the daily Examen provides a prayer structure that enables me to remember that my relationship with God needs intention, time, and attention each day, and that the experiences of my daily life direct me to know the ways that God calls me and forms me in my life as a Christian. Through the conscious practice and discipline of this prayer, I can better learn to recognize God's presence in my life, and I can be more discerning and responsible to God each day.[6]

An app that has helped me is Examen Prayer: detailed guidance for practicing this prayer. There is a tool for creating a daily journal of your reflections after praying the Examen.

The Examen Prayer need not be intricate or overwhelming . It is basically a way to reflect on yourself in God's presence. Two questions will get you started. As you look on this day, for what are you most grateful to God? As you look back on the events of your life: for what are you most grateful to God?

---

5. Martin, *Life with the Saints*, 354.

6. "Faith at Marquette," https://www.marquette.edu/faith/examen-of-consciousness.php.

Chapter Thirteen

Ways of Prayer for Men
Contemplative Prayer, Centering Prayer

When man is with God in awe and love, then he is praying. Then he doesn't perform everything at once, because it will never be possible for him, the finite, to do that in this life. But he is at least with him who is everything, and therefore he does something most important and necessary. Something not everyone does. For just because prayer belongs to the most necessary it is also the freest, the most avoidable, which only exists when we do it freely, always with new love, otherwise it would not exist.

—Karl Rahner[1]

This is the third day of a retreat at Mount Calvary Monastery, the Episcopal Benedictine retreat center in the foothills above Montecito, California. I have prayed several of the monastic offices with the monks, and have been to early morning Mass. In the late afternoon, before Vespers, I sit on a wooden bench in a garden, overlooking Rattlesnake Canyon. The shimmering Pacific Ocean is in the distance. The sun will set soon. A gentle breeze carries the scents of sage and juniper up from the canyon below. Creatures scurry about in the underbrush.

1. Rahner, *Need and Blessing of Prayer*, 1.

My mind is emptied of all the voices that chattered in my head as I drove one-hundred-fifty miles north to this retreat. Those voices are now mostly silent. I am listening to nature rustling around me, speaking in the rhythm of a day turning into night.

There is a warmth penetrating my body that is not of the sun. It fills my body with welcome heat, gentleness, sweetness. Is this what God's embrace of love and peace feels like? I let go of it, closing my eyes.

I do not fall asleep, but this encounter holds me tight to the bench in the garden. A bell rings in the distance; faint at first, then it becomes louder and clearer: the bell calling the monks to Vespers. I have been sitting for over an hour, but it seems like five minutes.

Hours later, lying on my bed in the monastic cell before sleeping, I remember this embrace of God. It was a visitation unconjured, unexpected and unmanipulated. The feeling of peace and love stayed with me in my sleeping hours.

Jesuit mystic Augustin Poulain writes about the prayer of quiet:

> This comes abruptly and unexpectedly. You are suddenly possessed by an unusual state of recollection which you cannot help but notice. You are overtaken by a divine wave that fills you through and through. You remain motionless beneath the influence of this sweet impression. And then it all disappears with the same suddenness. Beginners are surprised at this, for they find that they are overtaken by something that they cannot completely understand. But they surrender themselves to this inclination because they realize at once that it is something holy. They postpone to a later date the task of examining it more closely.[2]

Today, as I remember that experience on the prayer bench at the monastery, an image came to me: I had been on a bench at a bus stop waiting for the Holy Spirit to arrive. There is no schedule, therefore no expectation. But I had to show up for this encounter to happen.

I shared this experience with a friend. She asked me an important question: "How do you know you are really praying with God or just talking to yourself?" It is common when we pray to talk to ourselves instead of to God.

I have tried to approach my prayer with God in this way: I want to pray as if I am having an encounter with an actual person, which I am. I am speaking with God. I begin my prayers by asking God to be with me, to

---

2. Poulain, *Graces of Interior Prayer*, 200–201.

touch my heart, not just my mind. I ask God to remind me again that God loves and forgives me, as I love God.

The fifteenth-century Spanish Carmelite and mystic, Saint Teresa of Avila said, "A prayer in which a person is not aware of whom he/she is speaking to . . . I do not call prayer, however much the lips move."[3]

How do I know if God is talking to me in prayer? One way of knowing that I have found helpful is from the insight of Saint Ignatius Loyola: our experience of consolation, when God touches our soul and allows it to be comforted and strengthened by an awareness of God's love. Another way is after I have been praying about some important decision and a surprising, joyful answer to the prayer happens: I remember laughing out loud, looking out a window in our home, perhaps, and exclaiming: "Lord, you really are real. You do hear me!" And another way is when I am doing spiritual reading. Sometimes I read words that touch my heart deeply with an awareness of God's power and goodness.

I have this thought: does the discipline of faithfully praying portions of the Liturgy of the Hours and the Examen open our soul toward contemplative prayer? When I think of contemplative prayer, I remember one of the great spiritual masters, Thomas Merton, Trappist monk and author of the autobiographical *The Seven Storey Mountain*.

Every semester, when I taught the Christianity portion of my college class on world religions, I presented a powerful video on the life of Thomas Merton: *Merton: A Film Biography* (1984). In my class were many students who had not grown up in a spiritual tradition, but I found that this video was transformative for them. It connected with their own restless, searching souls.

Thomas Merton was a writer who was a typical "party animal" in his college days of the 1930s. Yet he had a holy longing that eventually led him to become a Trappist monk, one of the most austere forms of monasticism. He found serenity and deep connection with God in his practice of contemplative prayer.

As you read Merton's journals you see the restlessness, the holy longing were unremitting. After several decades at the monastery, he became the first Trappist monk given permission to become a hermit, living alone in a small cabin at the Abbey of Our Lady of Gethsemane in Kentucky. His restlessness pushed him to seek more isolated locations. He went to New Mexico, Arizona, and Northern California seeking the right spot.

3. Kavanaugh, *Wisdom of Teresa of Avila*, 33.

Father Thomas Keating, a fellow Trappist, would meet many young people who came to another monastery on retreat—St. Joseph's Abbey in Spencer, Massachusetts. Coming with experiences of Eastern mysticism and transcendental meditation, they had little understanding of Christian contemplative practices. To help these spiritual seekers for communion with God, Father Keating developed the specific technique of Centering Prayer.

Another Trappist monk, Father Basil Pennington, shares some steps for practicing this prayer form in his book *Centering Prayer.*[4]

1. Sit comfortably with your eyes closed, relax, and quiet yourself. Be in love and faith with God.

2. Choose a sacred word that best supports your sincere intention to be in the Lord's presence and open to His divine action within you.

3. Let that word be gently present as your symbol of your sincere intention to be in the Lord's presence and open to His divine action within you.

4. Whenever you become aware of anything (thoughts, feelings, perceptions, images, associations, etc.), simply return to your sacred word, your anchor. Let go of every kind of thought during prayer.

Merton was a master of world mystical traditions, but he took a different approach from his Trappist colleagues. He found that contemplative prayer was not a kind of altered state or blank consciousness, emptied of feeling and thought. There is no special technique to master in contemplative prayer. For Merton, contemplation is a way of being present to what is going on within ourselves. Father Ron Rolheiser helps us to understand this:

> We are in solitude, in contemplation, in prayer, when we feel the warmth of a blanket, taste the flavor of coffee, share love and friendship, and perform the everyday tasks of our lives so as to perceive in them that our lives are not little or anonymous or unimportant, but what is timeless and eternal is in the ordinary of our lives.[5]

I remember a story Father Rolheiser wrote about a man who had lost the will to pray. A Jesuit priest friend advised him to sit in silence every day

4. Pennington, *Centering Prayer*, xvi.
5. Rolheiser, "Contemplative Prayer," March 30, 2003.

for thirty minutes for six months. The man said he did not think this would work. But his friend urged him to "Just show up and sit in silent prayer, even if you are talking to a wall." Six months later, the man reconnected in faith with God.[6]

In 1999, I went through six hours of surgery at Cedars Sinai Hospital in Los Angeles, for a total colectomy, the removal of my large colon. My mother had died from colon cancer ten years earlier and my doctor advised that if I did not have this preventative surgery, I would have colon cancer within six months. For almost two weeks I languished in recovery, with many tubes coming out of my pain-wracked body. I could not pray. I existed within a grey cloud of pain-medicine and inability to keep food down. I would sit in the chair beside the bed for most of the night, staring at the wall, an empty void of nothingness. I could not pray. I did not care. I sat in long silence. Toward the end of that slow recovery, my eyes brightened in hope, and food stayed in my stomach. Janice told me about close friends who had been with me in the hospital room for hours at a time. I never saw them, but I did sense a presence. When I described my own times of depression and dark thoughts to my spiritual director, Father Gordon Moreland, when I might go days on end without being able to pray, I felt a presence with me, which I now know was the Lord's presence: like the patient, loving friends in the hospital room.

Please join me in spending fifteen minutes today in silent contemplation. Find a quiet place where you can do this. I drove one hundred and fifty miles to sit on a prayer bench at Mount Calvary Monastery. Thomas Merton searched and searched for the best place for solitude and silence for his contemplative prayer. The place where you choose to pray with the Lord is always the perfect place for you.

Here is more guidance from Father Ron Rolheiser, OMI, about resting in God's presence:

1. Find a place where you can sit quietly, comfortably, for fifteen minutes.

2. Here is a short Bible passage. "As the Father has loved me, so have I loved you. Now remain in my love."[7]

3. Close your eyes or focus on a candle flame or an icon. Imagine yourself in the presence of God, a God who yearns to be close to you. Some people find it helpful to silently repeat a simple word or phrase: Jesus,

6. Rolheiser, *Prayer: Our Deepest Longing*, 44–45.
7. John 15:9.

115

blessed be God, Hosanna, or Lord have mercy. If you worry you are not doing it right, listen to this advice given to me: "I just look at God, and I let God look at me."[8]

And when you have completed your contemplative time, you may wish to describe to yourself or your spiritual director a particular experience of God's love for you. In your contemplation what have you found that will help you in your prayer-friendship with God?

8. Rolheiser, "Resting in God's Presence," https://www.franciscanmedia.org/franciscan-spirit-blog/resting-in-gods-presence.

Chapter Fourteen

Why Are Women More Spiritual Than Men?

LET US NOW CONSIDER "the elephant in the sanctuary!" As you and I look over the faces of worshippers gathered on a Sunday in an American church, the majority will be women. Are women more spiritual and faithful to their religious traditions than men? Marta Trzebiatowska and her team of sociologists have seriously studied this question, revealing:

> Since 1945, the Gallup polling organization has consistently found that, on every index used, American women are more religious than men and not by small margins.[1]

The Pew Research Center, a nonpartisan fact tank in Washington, D.C., studies demographic trends and social issues. Recently, they published *The Gender Gap in Religion Around the World,* observing that "women are generally more religious than men, particularly among Christians."[2] In addition the report tells us: "In the United States, for example, women are more likely than men to say religion is 'very important' in their lives. American women also are more likely than American men to say they pray daily and attend religious services at least once a week." It then goes on to say:

1. Trzebiatowska and Bruce, *Why Are Women,* 6.
2. Pew Research Center, "Gender Gap in Religion Around the World," https://www.pewforum.org/2016/03/22/the-gender-gap-in-religion-around-the-world/.

A few sociologists have theorized that the gender gap in religion is biological in Nature, possibly stemming from higher levels of testosterone in men or other physical and genetic differences between the sexes. Christian women are more religious than Christian men . . . Christian women report praying daily more frequently than Christian men by an overall average gap of ten percentage points. . . . Scholars of religion have been examining possible reasons for the gender gaps: biology, psychology, family environment, social status, workforce participation and lack of 'existential security' felt by many women because they generally are more afflicted than men by poverty, illness, old age and violence.[3]

David Voas, head of the Department of Social Science at University College London, reflects on this report:

I'm not an expert in genetics, but there appears to be some fairly compelling evidence (for example, from studies of twins) that genes do affect our disposition to be religious. And if that's the case, it's at least plausible that the gender gap in religiosity is partly a matter of biology. If true, though, I doubt that it's because there's a 'God gene' and women are more likely to have it than men. It seems easier to believe that physiological or hormonal differences could influence personality, which may in turn be linked to variations in 'spirituality' or religious thinking.[4]

As America became more secularized, that is, without state support of religion after the 1820s, Tzrebiatowska reports that,

The division of the life-world into relatively distinct spheres initially insulated women from many of the secularizing forces that bore on the public sphere . . . (That) the home should be the primary site for religious edification and socialization seems to explain why secularization should have impacted on men earlier and to a greater extent than on women.[5]

Why do American men struggle with spirituality? We have inherited the values of critical thinking and science from the European Enlightenment of the seventeenth and eighteenth centuries. We now live in a secular

3. Pew Research Center, "Gender Gap in Religion Around the World," https://www.pewforum.org/2016/03/22/the-gender-gap-in-religion-around-the-world/.

4. Pew Research Center, "Why are Women Generally More Religious than Men?" https://www.pewresearch.org/fact-tank/2016/03/23/qa-why-are-women-generally-more-religious-than-men/.

5. Trzebiatowska and Bruce, *Why Are Women*, 165–66.

culture which is suspicious of religious experience and dogmatic theology. Religion can be defined as that which connects all of life together. In medieval Paris, France, for example, religion encompassed all aspects of daily life. There was no separation between the sacred and secular. Religious rituals were celebrated in a world of spiritual enchantment. This world view changed radically as early scientists sought knowledge in the book of nature rather than the dogma of the Bible. At a time when it was assumed that everyone believed in the Christian God, Rene Descartes (1596–1656) inspired the shift from religious orthodoxy to the primacy of the individual conscience.

German sociologist Max Weber described this process as the demystification of the modern world. Nature and the cosmos no longer invited mystical contemplation. Instead, they came to be seen as material systems to be studied. The emerging modern world required rational control. Descartes contended that creating a "buffered self" was the best defense against the siren call of old superstitions. The Canadian philosopher Charles Taylor writes,

> The buffered self is the agent who no longer fears demons, spirits, and magic forces. More radically, these no longer impinge; they don't exist for him; whatever threat or other meaning they proffer doesn't 'get it' from him.
>
> This super buffered self. . . is not only not 'got at' by demons and spirits; he is also utterly unmoved by the aura of desire. In a mechanistic universe, and in a field of functionally understood passion, there is no more room for such an aura. There is nothing it could correspond to. It is just a disturbing, supercharged feeling which somehow grips us until we can come to our senses and take on our full, buffered identity.[6]

Max Weber, in *The Protestant Ethic and the Rise of Capitalism,* describes how ambition, hard work, accumulation of capital, and the pieties of thrift and simplicity became spiritual virtues of the Protestant Reformation. Success in your profession may be evidence of God's blessing, your predestined salvation.

Even as Enlightenment values for reason, and Reformation values for the work ethic translated to the American colonies, each colony had its own established state church, supported by tax money. Each colony by law required all citizens to attend church services. Thomas Jefferson and

---

6. Taylor, *Secular Age,* 135.

James Madison, influential leaders in the American Revolution, affirmed the Enlightenment's teachings so that the Constitution of the United States expressed the radical idea that every person must be free to choose his or her spiritual path. No one was to be compelled to follow any religion in which they did not believe.

When these colonial, now state, churches were disestablished, men who provided their leadership lost status, which diminished interest in participation. Men who worked in government had to deal with people from different religious traditions. Men were more likely to travel extensively for their business or military service. These factors would also have diluted any sense of uniformity of religion and influenced men's disaffiliation.[7]

This process of disenchantment through the European Enlightenment, Protestant Reformation and the American Constitution, resulted in the reality that religion became purely a private matter in the United States.

Noting the contradistinction of the fire inside us for communion with God with the pursuit of success in the world, there has arisen a whole publishing industry speaking to masculine spirituality.

In the 1990s, the early book on the men's movement was Robert Bly's *Iron Man,* which sparked exploration of what is unique to men and their spirituality. Masculinity to Bly meant spontaneous wildness and taking risks. To awaken to Bly's ideal of the true self involves austere, elaborate initiation. Modern western culture has tamed and suppressed natural male instincts. Mythologies from different cultures give directional clues to an inward awakening. Was Bly countering the feminist critique of masculinity?

A best-selling book on Christian masculinity is John Eldredge's *Wild at Heart* (2001). After twenty years, the book continues to be number one on the subject of spirituality for men within evangelical Christianity. Eldredge, a Christian counselor, and lecturer, invites men to recover their masculine heart and return to "authentic masculinity," connecting with their deepest desires. I found kinship with Eldredge as he shares his own retreats in desert and mountain landscapes.

The book has three parts. Part One describes men as image-bearers of God. Men are made to "come through." As a man, do you have what it takes? Part Two contends all men carry a wound. We all carry a false self that we project to the outer world, expressed in extreme ways in anger or passivity. Healing comes if we bring those wounds to Jesus and recover a restored masculine heart. In Part Three, Eldredge describes the Core Desires

7. Trzebiatowska and Bruce, *Why Are Women,* 165.

of a Man's Heart: battle, adventure, beauty. Within the heart of every man is the heart of a warrior who wants to fight for something important and precious. Within the heart of every man is a longing for exploration and adventure connected to God's call. Within the heart of every man is a "beauty to rescue," to be found in nature, the arts, and in a personal relationship with God. We will find our deepest longings and desires in relationship with God. He asks important questions to his male readers: "Who am I? What am I made of? What am I destined for?"[8]

Richard Rohr, Franciscan priest and liberal Roman Catholic, represents the other end of the masculine spirituality spectrum. He has been much criticized by conservative Christians for his lack of orthodoxy—something he has in common with many spiritual mystics. In reading his books, *From Wild Man to Wise Man* and, *Falling Upward,* I can see influence from the analytical psychology of C.G. Jung, his emphasis on archetypes, common figures found in dreams and cross-cultural mythology as clues to the collective unconscious.

Professor Armin M. Kummer of the Catholic University of Leuven, Belgium, reflects:

> Rohr believes that most contemporary men possess no internal motivation. Their choices are driven by the external motivators, money, sex, and power. They are in the grasp of groupthink and other forms of social control that are opposed to individual consciousness and personal conscience. The traditional masculine enterprise of creating and producing has been replaced with making money as the primary goal in life. In Rohr's view, the contemporary willingness to dedicate life to the production of items of no social benefit has led to men's emotional stunting. Relational and social skills have withered because men live their lives at odds with their phallic energy, the masculine drive towards intercourse, and the beginning of life.[9]

Richard Rohr also contends that men carry a wound, which he calls "father wound," based on the absence of a man's father. If accumulation of wealth is a man's ultimate concern, there is little time to nurture relationships with children.

---

8. Eldridge, *Wild at Heart,* 5.

9. Kummer, *Men, Spirituality,* 18–19.

Rohr defines spirituality as "having a source of energy within which is a motivating and directing force for living."[10] This is similar to Rolheiser's definition of spirituality: how we channel that fire within us. Spirituality for men, according to Rohr, "would emphasize movement over stillness, action over theory, service to the world over religious discussions, speaking the truth over social niceties and doing justice instead of any self-serving 'charity.'"[11]

In his recent book *Falling Upward: A Spirituality for the Two Halves of Life*, Rohr considers the first half of a man's life, the restless pursuit of power, sex, and money, at the cost of one's inner self, creating an underdeveloped persona called *puer* (boy-child). In order to find our true self, the self that God implanted in us as our spiritual destiny, there is an unavoidable suffering that must come upon us. As you have read this book up to this point, you can hear my "Amen" to this.

Rohr writes about the false self and true self:

> Your False Self is your role, title, and personal image that is largely a creation of your own mind and attachments. It will and must die in exact correlation to how much you want the Real. . . . Your True Self is who you objectively are from the beginning, in the mind and heart of God. . . . It is your substantial self, your absolute identity, which can be neither gained nor lost by any technique, group affiliation, morality, or formula whatsoever. The surrendering of our false self, which we have usually taken for our absolute identity, yet is merely a relative identity, is the necessary suffering needed to find "the pearl of great price" that is always hidden inside this lovely but passing shell.[12]

Drawing on Eastern and Native American religious traditions, Rohr lifts up the role of mentor who can guide and teach a younger man, just as Jesus offered spiritual formation for his disciples.[13] And he encourages desert retreats of silence and solitude and contemplative prayer as resources for building friendship with God.

Contemporary writers on men's spirituality seem to be motivated by the diminished self-identity of men caused by the women's movement. I believe that a way forward for men in rediscovery of their spiritual selves will

10. Rohr and Martos, *Wild Man to Wise Man*, 36.

11. Rohr and Martos, *Wild Man to Wise Man*, 10.

12. Rohr, *Falling Upward*, 85–86.

13. Kummer, *Men, Spirituality*, 21.

be found in opportunities for connection with the spiritual lives of women. I have experienced this in two ways.

For forty years, I have shared ministry with the Sisters of Saint Joseph of Orange, a century-old Roman Catholic religious community in Orange, California. One of their charisms or spiritual gifts is public work for justice and peace. Sister Eileen McNerney, CSJ founded Taller San Jose in 1995 (St. Joseph's Workshop) as a response to increased gang violence, youth unemployment, low rates of high school graduation, and rising rates of teen pregnancy. The Hope Builders program enrolls two hundred young adults and helps them achieve and maintain self-sufficiency. Women and men receive training for employment in construction and medical services. I know that the contact with the Sisters by young men in the programs and business professionals who mentor or teach in the programs has stimulated their spiritual renewal. "Preach the gospel at all times, when necessary, use words." The Sisters of Saint Joseph, in their life-changing ministries of peace and justice, are visible testimonies to the joy of life with God.

Another ministry of the Sisters of Saint Joseph of Orange is the Center for Spiritual Development. Spiritual directors are trained at the Center, which also offers seminars on a wide-spectrum on spirituality for men and women who seek a deeper relationship with God. Men who may have no religious affiliation find a welcoming "side-door" for spiritual exploration.

A second experience for me of how women have enriched my spiritual life are the five women priests who have been my colleagues. As a self-driven alpha male, focusing on fund-raising for low-income early childhood centers, and an after school youth center, and growing the parish, the multi-tasking can take on a manic momentum. In close partnership with my female clergy colleagues, I had help with paying attention to relationships, conflict management, and taking time at staff meetings for prayer and scripture, reminding us for whom we are laboring. Before I would send an angry letter to the bishop or another party with whom I had disagreements, I learned to submit the letter to one of my female colleagues for editing or deletion. I found balance in my professional life and gratitude for the priesthood through shared ministry with these remarkable women.

As a man, passing through the eighth decade of life, I look back with regret and sorrow for things done and left undone. I see the faces of persons I have hurt, disappointed, and neglected. I remember bad choices that had serious life-changing consequences for me and those I loved. I remember addictive behaviors and the deceptive inner voice that urged me on: "You can do this; *you* are in control!" Thank God that I lived long enough to come to this place of contemplative reflection. Thank God for that awakening of the Spirit to help me see that, all along, in my frantic restless wanderings and hell-bent fixations, I was somewhere within my deepest self, seeking God. Thank God I had the help of Sister Jeanne Fallon, CSJ, and Father Gordon Moreland, SJ, to remind me as spiritual directors that I am God's beloved.

Lord God, my prayers do not conjure your presence. You have always been present throughout my life and I did not know this. You are present everywhere for everyone. The problem has been me being present to you.

The awakening I experienced of God's love for me and all creation came at the end of praying through the Spiritual Exercises of Saint Ignatius Loyola for a year with Sister Jeanne. At the end of that year, she guided me through the Contemplation to Attain Divine Love. I remember that there are four parts:

1. Remember how much God has done for me.

2. Think about the way God "dwells in all living things and in me, created in God's image."

3. Consider how God cares for and nurtures creation.

4. Consider how God inspires us to work for justice and mercy in the world as his active presence.

On our last day of that year together, Sister Jeanne invited me to pray the *Suscipe* Prayer, a prayer of self-surrender of my life to God, acknowledging that all I need to thrive and serve in this life is God's love and grace.

> Take, Lord, and receive all my liberty,
> my memory, my understanding, and all my will---
> all that I have and possess.
> You, Lord, have given all that to me.
> I now give it back to you, O Lord.
> All of it is yours.
> Dispose of it according to your will.
> Give me love of yourself along with grace,
> for that is enough for me.[14]

You and I, in our desire for deeper connection with Jesus, find a helpful brother in Augustine of Hippo, the bishop from North Africa, and his

---

14. Martin, *Jesuit Guide to (Almost) Everything*, 396–97.

autobiographical *Confessions* (circa AD 400). By that time, Christianity had been legalized in the Roman Empire, the age of physical martyrdom was over and the spiritual work for Christians had become an inner struggle. Some men and women took to the deserts of Palestine, Syria, and Egypt to seek solitude, silence, and contemplation with God. Listening to Augustine's voice as I read the *Confessions,* I recognize a person praying to God, like the voice I hear of the psalmist in the Bible. For thirty-four years of his life, Augustine searched restlessly for meaning and fulfillment in the world. His intense intellectual mind drew him to be a rabid devotee of various Greek philosophies and cults, an ardent lover of women, and ambitious in his teaching career—receiving an academic appointment from the Roman Emperor himself. A desire for God moved within him, but he thought this restless activity in the world had nothing to do with that. The journey inward was not self-initiated.

He was in a garden, thinking about thinking and the way God works, when he was surprised to hear a child's voice chanting "Take up and read, take up and read." He opens a book to Paul's Letter to the Romans: "Let us behave decently, as in the daytime, not in carousing and drunkenness, not in sexual immorality and debauchery, not in dissension and jealousy. Rather, clothe yourselves with the Lord Jesus Christ, and do not think about how to gratify the desires of the flesh."[15]

With clarity of mind, heart, and soul, he chooses baptism and Jesus Christ as his Lord and Savior. Augustine of Hippo joins you and me in awakening to the knowledge that we are beloved sons of God. This is where a man who struggles with his life with God must begin. Augustine prays for all of us as he says to the Lord: "You are good and all-powerful, caring for each one of us as though each is the only one in your care."[16]

15. Romans 13:13–14.
16. Augustine, *Confessions*, 50.

Chapter Fifteen

Where is Jan in All This?

> Most of us grow up only during a marriage or a work-life or a
> sweeping self-examination, not before then.
>
> — David Whyte[1]

WHEN SHE WAS PREPARING the foreword for this book, Sister Eileen Mc-
Nerney surprised me when she asked, "Where is Jan in all of this? What
has it been like being a man who is a priest and married?" These insightful
questions sparked reflection as I approach the fiftieth anniversary of ordination to the priesthood and our fiftieth wedding anniversary.

In my early twenties, contemplating marriage, I had the haunting pre-
monition that a terrible storm would break into my life and if so, I needed
a strong partner to stand with me.

I was twenty-five when I began ministry at St. Mary's Episcopal
Church in Laguna Beach, California. Janice was already living in that sea-
side town. In 1968, she had left her home in Shrewsbury, Massachusetts,
where her family roots reach back to the pilgrims. A newly-licensed reg-
istered nurse, she headed west in her sky-blue Volkswagen, her only companion a chocolate-brown toy poodle. After two months of adventuring
she arrived at the home of her cousin Rosemary in the industrial port of
Long Beach. Then one day she drove a few miles south on Pacific Coast

---

1. Whyte, *Three Marriages*, 22.

Highway, and came across the bohemian artist's colony of Laguna Beach in all its stunning beauty. Janice visited the local hospital and had a walk-in interview. They hired her on the spot.

I first saw her, a beautiful brunette nurse in the intensive care unit, while I was praying with a critically ill parishioner—a jarring conjunction of the sacred and profane. Two months later I attended a Human Relations Institute workshop on communications for a week. Janice was in my small group, and so it began.

As we look back on that first year of our dating, we have contrasting perspectives. I was in love, convinced that she was the one. But she would back away from the onslaught of my attentions. That first year involved several separations, during which I had to admit that we were going nowhere. Then I realized that if I were able to be more detached I would become less threatening to her. The relationship indeed blossomed and we married on the 27th of November, 1971.

We both had professions into which we poured our hearts. Janice became head nurse of the emergency department at the Laguna Beach hospital, where she came to spend most of her long career. Ministry at St. Mary's with Father Bob challenged me because I had also begun part-time work as associate professor of philosophy at Saddleback Community College. Daughter Katie was born in 1976 and the juggling act of parenting and work became intense. Janice changed to the 3–11pm shift. But with childcare and carefully coordinated work schedules, our dynamic life flowed.

When I studied marriage and family counseling in seminary, the professor discussed the "seven-year itch"—the real thing, not the 1955 film starring Marilyn Monroe. Research has determined that happiness in a marriage lessens after seven years,[2] and the median duration of a marriage is seven years.[3]

On cue, in our seventh year of marriage, conflict and depression threatened our future. We both sought counseling, and at one point we separated. I left on sabbatical to study with the theologian Hans Küng in Tübingen, Germany. To leave then was really stupid, but off I went. Paralyzing depression seized me when I arrived in Germany. Very early, one overcast morning in Leipzig (in my estimation the bleakest city in communist

---

2. "Ties that Unbind," *Psychology Today*, https://www.psychologytoday.com/us/articles/200001/the-ties-unbind.

3. "National Vital Statistics," *U. S. Department of Health and Human Services.*

East Germany) a voice said: Wake up! What the hell are you doing here? Go home now!

Two days later I was back in Orange County. The anger and reactivity of the past year, fed by a feeling that the other was not the perfect person we each needed, softened. We both reached a resolution that we must make peace with the imperfections in each other and no matter what, remain together as a family. God's grace somehow led us to this unexpected place in our marriage as a preparation for the storm that was coming.

In 1981, when I became Rector of the Episcopal Church of the Messiah in Santa Ana, the century-old parish was accustomed to having the rector's spouse serve as an unpaid assistant, providing leadership for women's ministries. However, it was very clear that Janice's ministry was in the ER where she cared for dying patients during the HIV-AIDS epidemic. The parish adapted to this change.

Our son Erik was born on June 6, 1983. A handsome boy. Ten days later, Janice was sitting on the couch in the living room when Erik had a slight tremor. A seizure? We went to the ER and Erik was admitted to Pediatric ICU with encephalitis. The doctors committed a major medical error by not doing a TORCH screen, which would have determined the cause of the brain disease. Erik was discharged after his fever subsided. After that there were some developmental issues to deal with, but our busy working lives continued.

Every summer Janice and I, and later, our children, flew to Boston for a month's vacation in her family home in a classic New England village one hour west of Boston. There we could both detox from our adrenaline-driven lives and become fully present to one another. On our first mornings there, I would walk groggily a few blocks to the village center to buy the *New York Times*. I had to be there before nine-thirty for by then they would be sold out. Once I asked the shopkeeper why he didn't bring in more copies, "I would just have to sell more papers," he replied. Nothing changes in Shrewsbury.

I recall taking little Erik up to the old Shrewsbury High School football field. I booted the soccer ball as far as I could. He would run like crazy, turn around and dribble it back, kicking a goal between my legs. At three years old, he was fleet of foot and tireless.

Life changed on June 16, 1987. On the flight to our vacation Erik seized and the convulsions would not stop. The paramedics wheeled him off the plane, past his grandparents who were expecting to give us a joyful welcome. After hours in the ER at Massachusetts General Hospital, they admitted Erik and Jan and I found a room at the Parker House Hotel. Katie went with her grandparents back to Shrewsbury. I remember how Jan and I held on to each other as this unbelievably dreadful storm looked as though it might take the life of our son. That is all you can do, hold on to each other tightly and pray to the Lord.

All that month Erik was in an out of coma, near death. The encephalitis of infancy had returned. Without the TORCH Screen test when he was ten days old, it was a guessing game. Meanwhile, the disease burned through his brain like a California wildfire. Later, it was determined that the cause was herpes. If we had known that beforehand, the brain damage could have been avoided.

Over the next thirty years, Janice and I continued in our professions. While daughter Katie flourished at Saint Margaret's Episcopal School in San Juan Capistrano, we had to battle the local school district to get special education for Erik. One thing I learned about school districts: state law required them to provide special education, but a parent must learn the secret words to gain access. Our family therapist happened to be Director of Special Education for the Irvine School District and coached us on the access codes.

Janice had a dream that seemed unattainable, given the circumstances. As a highly experienced nurse-director of emergency medicine, she wanted to become a family nurse practitioner, a then-evolving profession that enabled nurses to prescribe medication and to have a clinical practice similar to physicians. I urged her to apply to the program at California State University Dominguez Hills. She progressed, one semester after another, while working full time in the ER. We would hit a wall every time Erik had to go into the hospital, but I urged her on.

I remember one Holy Week when Erik was in the hospital, Janice and I alternated sleeping in his room. Janice worked on her master's thesis there one night, on the next I slept there, got up early and went off to preside at the Good Friday service. It was like that, night after night.

At about this time I was beginning my long acquaintance with spiritual direction. After twenty-seven years with Father Gordon Moreland, SJ, I continued direction with Father Domenico de Raimondo, MSPS. In October 2021, Father Domenico suggested that Janice join me at my next appointment with him. When we arrived at the House of Prayer, he led us through the chapel where mass is celebrated, the Blessed Sacrament

Chapel, and to the winding trail reserved for priests on retreat, where there were stations for contemplation and for praying the rosary. It felt strange to me having a woman's presence at a retreat center for celibate Catholic priests. I think in these first sessions Father Domenico wanted to encounter me as a married priest, hence the invitation to Janice.

We sat together in the warm ambience of the common-room library. Father Domenico asked each of us three questions about our life together. "What have been God's gifts to you in married life together? What do you admire in each other? What are you grateful for in each other?" Janice responded then, of course, and later wrote down her reflections. Here are her words:

> I recently had the pleasure of a visit with Brad's spiritual director. During the visit, he asked each of us: What are God's gifts to you in your married life, and what makes you grateful for the other? He also wanted us to reflect on how our relationship carried over into Brad's work, my work, and our church life.
>
> I had previously briefly attended Alanon meetings and was trying to follow their basic tenets of accepting things that I cannot change about Erik's condition, changing the things I can, by working to become more educated, to help him reach whatever could be his full potential, and with God's Help, to gain the wisdom to know the difference.
>
> Brad attended Adult Children of Alcoholics meetings for a while, and I saw him begin to work on acceptance too. So, we worked together to accept and be grateful for our damaged son, who was still loved by God. God loved him, because God sent many angels to help us along the way: an educational psychologist, neurologists, teachers, caregivers, social workers, a sister who loved and helped to care for her brother, and a wonderful, loving church family. Surrounded by God's love, and the love of others, Erik has become a gentle, happy, funny man-child. Together, Brad and I learned not only to accept Erik as he is, but to be thankful for the love and grace that surround all of us in his presence. Erik exudes a simple joy that people recognize. God's love emanates from him every day, and people recognize it.
>
> God's great gift to Brad and I in our married life has been to help us band together with family and friends in tough times, in loving support and encouragement, to help us be grateful for all the angels sent to surround us with love and hope in our lives together. Erik's weakness and fallibility have strengthened us. In allowing us to care for Erik's weakness, we have been allowed to gather our

strengths, our courage, our tenacity, in caring for him. I know these qualities have carried over in my life as a nurse and nurse practitioner and nursing educator, caring for our most vulnerable populations for over fifty years. It has clearly carried over in Brad's ministry to his congregation and the most vulnerable populations in Santa Ana.

I am grateful for Brad's ministry over the past fifty years. Brad has become a responsible steward of the resources of the church in sharing his understanding that the church's time, talents, and treasures could reach out into the community, especially to the most vulnerable populations. He has always believed in God's call to open the doors of the church and to welcome all who enter, but more, to walk out the door into the community, and become involved with other churches, community leaders, and advocates in responding to those many needs. All within the church have been encouraged to respond to the need. The result of saying 'yes' to that call has enabled a dying church to grow and become a shining beacon of hope within the community. The people of the church created programs to help vulnerable children grow and thrive, and developed programs to support and educate adults. They became involved in creating after-school tutoring programs, childcare centers for the area's most impoverished, and a program for preschool homeless children and their mothers. Then there was the startup of the St. Joseph Ballet that gives underprivileged youth confidence and strength. They opened their doors to several Alcoholics Anonymous and Alanon groups, Orange County High School for the Arts, the Catholic Worker group that cooked the food and fed the homeless in the courtyard—to name a few of the ministries supported by Messiah. The church family grew with people who supported these programs, or were involved with them, or who were recipients of services, from diverse backgrounds and cultures. By opening the doors, this diverse "hospital for sinners" became amazing! I am grateful for Brad's commitment and courage throughout his ministry.

And here are my own (Brad's) responses to Father Domenico's questions:

> Together and with God's amazing grace, step by step, we stood together in the Storm of Erik's many crises. When one of us was down and overwhelmed, the other seemed to rise. I am grateful for the gift of our challenging and fulfilling professions, serving people in the name of Jesus. As Rabbi Kushner said, people were truly God's language. God gifted us with medical resources,

therapists, teachers, anti-seizure drugs, and friends, all of which helped our family through the tough times. I am grateful for what I have learned about being patient and supportive of Janice.

I admire Jan's courage and skill in the emergency room, her focused presence with people, and her compassion. She never knew what was coming next: a teenager with a drug overdose, a surfer who needed suturing after colliding with the surfboard, a famous symphony conductor who was hyperventilating, a hungry homeless person with a fever, a frightened child with an infected foot, and victims from a horrific auto accident on Pacific Coast Highway right in front of the hospital. For twenty-five years she also taught nursing at Saddleback Community College. Hundreds of nursing students in her on-site hospital clinical classes learned how to give efficient, competent and compassionate care to everyone.

I am grateful for her support during my own two cancer treatments and her knowledge of the medical processes. I am grateful that we are both deeply committed to care for Erik. We won't give up.

Over the past fifty years, I have celebrated and blessed the marriages of over six-hundred couples. While there is insight about what sustains a life-long marriage, the reality is a mystery. In the late 1970s I blessed the marriage of a "hippie" couple, flowers in the hair, driving a rainbow-painted VW bus. They ended up living in Tennessee, with five children. The husband became a successful insurance salesman, the wife an elementary school teacher, and they send me a Christmas card every year. Another couple, sophisticated, graduate-school educated, broke up within a year. Episcopal clergy are required to provide premarital counseling, and my graduate degree is in pastoral care. We do personality inventories to help couples look at their differences and we talk about conflict resolution. I offer a warranty that when I bless a marriage, I am there for the couple when they need support and I tell them my own story of separation and recovery. Yet, it all comes down to work and grace. The work is what we must do with each other in learning about communication, honesty, trust and wishing the best for the other before we have it for ourselves. There will always be storms, insurmountable walls, impossible situations, when left to our own efforts, we will fail. Having a life with God and a religious community accesses the amazing grace that penetrates hopelessness, despair, and sorrow.

At the nuptial mass we pray: "Give them wisdom and devotion in the ordering of their common life, that each may be to the other a strength in need, a counselor in perplexity, a comfort in sorrow and a companion in joy."[4]

Janice, Father Brad and Erik, Mammoth Lakes, California 2019.
Author's Collection.

4. *BCP*, 429.

Chapter Sixteen

Embracing Joy

I have told you this so that my joy may be in you and that your joy
may be complete.

—JOHN 15:11

SATURDAY MORNING, BRILLIANT SUNSHINE, 75°F. Our son Erik and I begin
our walk around the big block. I hold on to his upper arm to steady him
as we begin the climb up the street that encircles our neighborhood. Erik
is alert with his supersonic hearing, responding to every distant sound: a
dog barking, a leaf-blower, a car door closing, a baby crying. He laughs and
repeats nonsense phrases. He kicks at a wall, stomps on a dried sycamore
leaf, thrusts his leg out toward a bush, laughing. Erik is alive with joy, living
only in this present moment.

Erik especially enjoys stepping into the recess in a lawn where the
concrete cap of the water meter is set. I tell Erik, "Now don't step into that
hole." He heads right for it, steps into the hole and laughs. We repeat this
at least a dozen times as we walk the one-mile of the big block, up hills and
down hills.

Erik is thirty-seven years old, but mentally four. That is the age when
encephalitis ravaged his brain. I look back to when I was thirty-seven, the
pastor of a busy urban parish, propelled by caffeine and the prioritized
daily task list in the Franklin Planner. My mind frantically moved in all

directions, lamenting an overdue project from yesterday, anxious about a critical board meeting tomorrow. There was no Now, least of all a joyful Now. As I experience walking beside our son in these, my retirement years, I can give myself fully to being present with him, relishing his robust joy at being right here now with me.

Last month I shared with my spiritual director, Father Gordon, a nagging issue. "I am looking back on my life with deep regrets about my behavior toward people I have wounded. A dark, judgmental energy has been haunting me, causing me to blurt out, 'I am sorry! I was so stupid!'"

Fr. Gordon responded, "Whoever comes to mind, pray that they will experience a surge of joy from the Lord."

He expanded that counsel with a more radical spirit:

"The people in your life who have died: let them know you are praying for them to have a surge of joy. For the Unfaithful Departed, help them let go of their capital sins (greed, lust, envy, etcetera) and embrace the joy of the Lord. For notorious criminals: pray that they will experience a surge of joy from the Lord."

I remember that Father Gordon expanded this counsel in one of his Christmas letters:

> The Divine Trinity is the very personification of love. This is the love of God, Father, Son, Holy Spirit. The three persons of the Trinity is also an extravaganza of joy. And that joy diffuses itself by being poured forth into creation. Most especially the Trinity create other persons to share that joy. And we as human beings are the recipients of that joy. Jesus made two things pretty clear; He wanted us to share His joy and he wants our joy to be complete. This is what God wants of us, as Saint Paul proclaims in Philippians, "Rejoice always. Again, I say rejoice." (Philippians 4:4)
>
> Praying for the eternal happiness of all people means I no longer have enemies, because I no longer carry the heavy burden of resentment toward anyone. At the least, I unburden myself and I am liberated to make room to welcome joy.[1]

Joy is central to our life with each other and with God.

On the one-year anniversary of the breakout of COVID-19 virus, I am waiting in line at Albertson's supermarket (six feet behind the person in front of me). They are out of Lysol wipes, paper towels and toilet-paper again. Everyone is wearing masks. I look at the people around me, faces

---

1. Moreland, SJ, personal correspondence.

mostly covered, pushing shopping carts, heads down, a mother trying to herd a brood of school-age children who cannot attend school. There is no joy here, only the daily grind, trying not to get sick, trying to pay bills, trying to help children keep up with schoolwork.

Saint Patrick's Day is a couple of weeks away. In past years, celebrators would pack the restaurant, Irish jigs playing as gallons of Guinness pour from wooden kegs. Perhaps the virus census will improve so that bars and restaurants can open again. Festive celebrations, vacations, reunion with family and friends can foster joy once again. But a day or so after the event, we return to routine, ordinary time.

I remember this: a mid-morning hike on a cow trail along Olancha Creek, climbing westward toward the snow-covered Sierra Nevada mountains. In the early days of spring, an icy wind blows down from the mountains. Olancha Creek is dry as a bone, easy to cross to the other side. Enormous granite boulders and coarse gravel litter the landscape. The cow trail makes it easier to negotiate dense, scratchy Great Basin sage and spindly creosote.

Sweat trickles into my eyes. My breathing is labored as I climb, one step in front of the other. The mind slows into No Mind. Then the sound. I stop suddenly. Listen! Water flowing over rocks. I continue climbing, move back toward Olancha Creek, which is suddenly gushing with water!

I see a large, flat rock and collapse on it for a rest. On the ground beside my hiking shoes, I see black obsidian chips. A Paiute once sat on this rock to chip an arrowhead. Where I am hiking was once a substantial settlement of the Paiute people.

My breath and heart rate return to normal. In this moment, I am filled with a surge of well-being. In this desolate, desert place, on this rock, gratitude pours out for my family, my friends, the priesthood, the gift of being here. My heart fills with thankfulness to God.

This is genuine joy! It is more than a feeling. The sudden awareness becomes an open door to my heart to invite the Lord to be with me.

I cannot make joy happen. Joy visits us as part of the life we have been living.

The spiritual writer and monk, Ron Rolheiser gives us this:

> Joy is always the by-product of something else. As the various versions of The Prayer of Saint Francis put it, we can never attain joy, consolation, peace, forgiveness, love and understanding by actively pursuing them. We attain them by giving them out. That

is the great paradox at the center of all spirituality and one of the great foundational truths within the universe itself: The air that we breathe out is the air we will eventually breathe back in. Joy will come to us if we set about actively trying to create it for others.[2]

The sixteenth-century Spanish mystic and Carmelite, John of the Cross, also gives this counsel in this poem:

To reach satisfaction in all
desire its possession in nothing.
To come to possess all
desire the possession of nothing.
To arrive at being all
desire to be nothing.
To come to the knowledge of all
desire the knowledge of nothing.
To come to the pleasure you have not
you must go by the way in which you enjoy not.
To come to the knowledge you have not
you must go by a way in which you know not.
To come to the possession you have not
you must go by a way in which you possess not.
To come to be what you are not
you must go by a way in which you are not.[3]

This is the way to joy.

2. Rolheiser, "Meditation on Joy," https://ronrolheiser.com/a-meditation-on-joy/#.YS_GhY5KjE4.

3. John of the Cross, *Ascent of Mount Carmel*, 78.

Chapter Seventeen

Home Is Right Here!

More than anything else, we long for home. Our deep ache for intimacy, security, and comfort is, in the end, a longing for home, nothing more. We are forever restlessly searching for someone or something to take us home.

—RON ROLHEISER, OMI[1]

THE HUGE, ORANGE OCTOBER moon rises above the Sangre de Cristo Mountains. Soft light streams through the window of our travel trailer onto the face of our sleeping son. Gusts of gentle wind rustle piñon pine branches in the dense forest surrounding us, five miles east of Santa Fe, New Mexico.

Erik's childlike face reflects peace and serenity. I sleep next to him on the sofa-bed because during this night he will have a seizure, not as bad as those of years ago, but strong enough to wake me to keep him from falling out of bed. My wife Janice and I surround Erik in a circle of love, in this mobile home in which we have traveled these past three weeks.

In the morning, after breakfast, I walk with Erik on a forest trail. I must hold on to his hand, as he can easily trip. He likes to walk, and the morning mist is perfumed with piñon pine scent. We walk around a bend in the path, and I can see our trailer in the distance.

---

1. Rolheiser, "Home—the Place from Which to Understand," https://ronrolheiser.com/home-the-place-from-which-to-understand/#.YkZpBCjMLE4.

"Erik, where is our home? Is home our house in Laguna Niguel, or is our home that trailer over there?" Without missing a beat, Erik points to the ground of the space between us, responding,

"Home is right here!"

Home is right here, in this place where we stand, hand in hand, in the circle of love and care. Home is right here!

On another day, I am driving alone on the 210 Freeway through Arcadia, towards my hometown of Pasadena. The off-ramp passes over the site of our first family home. I drive three blocks north, toward the Sierra Madre Mountains, to the site of our second family home. There is a warm, visceral feeling that hits me as I drive through these familiar streets, imbedded with deep memories. At Mayfair Drive, I turn left. Halfway down the street I pull over under a gnarled, bent linden tree to catch sight of our old family home. Here was home.

My father, now ninety-six, sold the home years ago after the death of my mother and moved to a mobile-home village in Huntington Beach. Other families now call the old place home.

I have dreamed of this old home over the years since my father moved. At first, the vivid dreams brought me to the house. I would use my key, open the side door, and walk in, as I did in the past when I visited my dad. Suddenly, I see strange faces and I chastise myself for disturbing the family. I have had this dream for many years.

Now that my dad is nearing the end of life, the dream has changed. In the last year, at least twice a month, I dream that my dad still owns it but does not live there. In the dream, I am visiting the home with my dad and there are squatters living there. The plumbing does not work, paint peels from the walls, but it is still home. Frequently, my deceased mother appears in the dream, and we hug and talk as if she has been away somewhere. In successive dreams, I see more deterioration of the house, more damage; the roof is falling in. How strange the journeys of our unconscious! One friend suggested I am going through some early grief about the end of life of my father. Yet when I go to the old house in my dream or in an actual drive-by sighting, I feel I have arrived at home.

In all the twists and turns of my life up to the first years of marriage, travels in and out of state and in and out of the country, this house on Mayfair Drive was home. It was where I experienced unconditional love and I always felt that no matter how many mistakes I made in life, I had a welcome there.

I know that as you read this, you are remembering your own experiences of home—and for many people they are not pleasant memories. One priest colleague with whom I worked for many years had to move every two years, because her father was an Army chaplain.

Where do you and I find home?

There is a deep longing within each of us for something, some place, someone where we will experience love, joy, peace, and hope. Some will believe they can create that place through success, accomplishment, and money. However, the Buddha warns us that all such "homes," even if we are fortunate to arrive at that place in our life, are illusory and temporary. All that we hold dear will eventually pass from us. Home is in this present moment, this present breath. As Erik reminds me, home is right here.

Father Ron Rolheiser shares another answer:

> Home is a place in the heart, not a bloodline, building, city, or ethnicity. Home is that deep, fragile place where we hold and guard what's most precious to us. It's that place where, in some dark way, we remember that once, before we came to awareness, we were caressed by hands far gentler than any we've met in this life and where we were once kissed by a truth and a beauty so perfect that they are now the unconscious standard by which we measure everything. Home is where things 'ring true,' where what's most precious to us is cherished, the place of tender conscience, of intimacy.[2]

That foundational, innate memory of God's loving embrace and kiss is our homing-beacon. For the past two years, Janice, our son Erik, and I have been attending St. Timothy's Roman Catholic Church, two blocks from our home in Laguna Niguel. I have been an Episcopal priest for forty-four years and not a Roman Catholic, but our family began to attend the Sunday evening youth mass. The pastor, Monsignor John Urell, is a good friend. That friendship and proximity guided us to the church.

I worked hard as a pastor for forty-three years, mostly within the challenges of the Latino barrio congregation in Santa Ana. Three Masses every Sunday, incredible multitasking! Now in retirement, in this contemplative period of my life, I have experienced a sense of spiritual homecoming at St. Timothy's. How would I describe it? The words and music that draw the soul deeper into communion with God; Monsignor John's contemplative

2. Rolheiser, "Home," https://ronrolheiser.com/home-the-place-from-which-to-understand/#.YPCBhuhKjE4.

homilies full of his own honest walk with the Lord and hope and encouragement. At the time of communion, I am often brought to tears with a powerful embrace of the Holy Spirit. I look around and the voice within me says, "I am home." The Episcopal Church and the Roman Catholic Church share many similarities, including the liturgy of the Eucharist. The Roman Catholic Church does not have open communion to non-Catholics and out of respect for this, I do not take the sacrament. We do receive a blessing from the priest at communion, but still Janice and I agree, *this is home.* Not necessarily the building or the congregation, but in the words, music, aesthetics of liturgy, a doorway opens into a place in our heart. I am grateful for this grace and gift.

I walk in desert space somewhere in New Mexico near sunset. There is an unique way the sun sets there: the sky above the horizon tinted yellow, crimson and finally purple. The air is still and dry, perfumed with sage, juniper, and pine. There is stillness in Nature before darkness covers the landscape. My skin prickles, not a chilly wind, but some invisible touch, God's enveloping embrace. I feel it and I am home.

Chapter Eighteen

Wild Fears

[Kids aged three to eight should be taken] to visit field, forest, hill, shore, the water, flowers, animals, the true home of childhood. . . for the very soul and body cry out for a more active, objective life, and to know Nature and man at first hand. These two staples, stories, and Nature, by these informal methods of the home and the environment constitute fundamental education.

—G. STANLEY HALL, 1906.[1]

Americans find ourselves in a period—arguably, the first in our nation's history—when our unease about being in Nature is coming to outweigh our desire for it. We have a growing intolerance for inconvenience, a feeling well captured by the suburban fifth grader who memorably told Nature advocate Richard Louv, "I like to play indoors better 'cause that is where the electrical outlets are."

—GARY FERGUSON[2]

A COLD DECEMBER GUST gathers embers from a campfire of bleached mesquite, swirling them into a glowing column, which climbs into the crisp,

1. Hall, *Youth: Its Education, Regimen and Hygiene,* 4.
2. Ferguson, "Great Fear of the Great Outdoors," *Los Angeles Times,* December 21, 2014.

clear night sky, toward the enormous orange moon. I stand in a circle with my buddies of Boy Scout Troop 374 from Pasadena, California. We are camping in the Calico Mountains, in the Mojave Desert, east of Barstow and one hundred miles from home. We turn our bodies toward the warmth. I gaze out over rolling hills of sagebrush and creosote. There are no other people within ten miles.

I have a vivid memory of seeing that night the Aurora Borealis, the Northern Lights. Very rare, this far south. The scoutmaster pointed us toward the North Star, and there it was, radiating bands of crimson, violet and purple.

As the fire died out, I retreated to a tent and warm sleeping bag. I moved my hips about to create comfortable space. No air mattresses in those days. A band of coyotes sang to the moon in the distance.

A few weeks later, I spend my Saturday in a vast, wild field of oaks and pepper trees next to the main line of the Santa Fe Railroad. My brother Michael and I are stacking the walls of a tumbleweed fort. Soon, neighboring boys and girls from the street above will show up for another dirt-clod fight. For most of my childhood until junior high school, my brother and I were free to wander in desolate fields which we filled with rich imaginations. Mustard weeds grew six feet high then, and we made winding mazes among them.

These are some of the foundational experiences that helped me to feel happily at home in wild places. Yet, as I have been writing about wild, desert places over the past twenty years, I have come to understand that while being alone in a wilderness can appeal to some people, it can be a frightening nightmare for others.

On a clear, windless November afternoon, I am hiking an old Paiute trail into Sacatar Canyon, west of Highway 395, a few miles north of Little Lake, California. The trail climbs toward the Sierra Nevada mountains, on the north side of a stream filled with lush riparian vegetation: wild grape, willow, and canyon phacelia—a lavender flower. Autumn has turned the foliage gold and red. Black obsidian chips shine in the sunlight, evidence of Paiute tool-making. I pass a circle of stones, remains of a Paiute settlement and a collapsing tin-roofed miner's cabin. There are two animal prints in the soft sand of the trail: three inches wide with four toes and heel pad. Looks like mountain lion. There are enough recent deer droppings in the area to support that idea. An hour before the sun sets dark shadows fill the canyon. I am captivated by the quiet and sit on a granite boulder to contemplate this beautiful place. Suddenly, I hear a shrieking scream. Not a human one, but a sound I have heard before in nature videos: the cry of a mountain lion? I thought I saw the golden yellow face of a large cat moving in a thicket of willow upstream. Fear grabs me, my mouth runs dry, and I shift to run out of there. But I remember that animals sense fear, and running identifies me as prey. I stand on the boulder, making myself as large as I can, waving my jacket, shouting loud sounds, and throwing rocks in the direction of the cry. This activity calmed me as I slowly backed down the trail, turning again to throw more rocks toward that sound.

A hot June day, one hundred degrees. I drive toward the Reward Mine, in the Inyo Mountains east of Manzanar and Highway 395. As the sun sets, the temperature drops and a strong wind blows. I walk toward a stone miner's cabin that I have visited before. The still bright sun and dark shadows filling the rocky slope make it difficult to see what is in front of me. I know the way and am almost at the doorway of the old rock cabin when I hear the frightening sound: rattlesnake! Warning rattles from a snake somewhere near the entrance to the cabin. The shock throws me backwards and I roll down the slope, missing cholla cactus and a bite from the snake.

After a rainy night, I drive a sandy desert road on a blustery December morning towards the remains of the 1860s mining village of San Carlos, along the Owens River, east of Independence, California. I have visited the site many times, exploring the adobe brick foundations of defunct businesses, mills, and homes. Thick sagebrush, willow and salt grass have grown up over the town site. Suddenly, I hear a crashing sound in the distant brush coming up from the river and I see a huge Black Angus bull, with long, pointed horns pacing towards me, snorting, pawing the earth, shaking his head back and forth. I slowly back up to my car, get behind it, crawl inside, and look through the rearview mirror to see the bull returning into the dense underbrush.

Spiritual writer and desert pilgrim Belden Lane cautions us as we romanticize wilderness encounters:

> From the safety of our cubicles, we idealized a pristine wilderness of peaceful serenity (available to the wealthy in carefully-guarded five-star resorts) or we dwell on sensational images of wild animals tearing each other to bloody bits. We romanticize wilderness, on the one hand, and demonize it on the other. Bucolic images of 'getaway' places soothing the soul vie with Weather Channel depictions of an outrageously violent world. Either way, wilderness becomes a mythic construct, removed from any actual, intimate,

or ethical relationship to the land. Our immersion in the image inevitably makes possible our destruction of the reality.[3]

I am on an eight-day silent retreat at Mount Calvary Monastery, the Anglican monastic community in the foothills high above Santa Barbara. The old Spanish-styled hacienda with a central garden-patio and a dozen guest rooms includes a refectory that would fit right into a medieval monastery in Europe. There is a long, antique dining-table surrounded by eighteenth-century Spanish chairs. The chapel, where the Liturgy of the Hours is prayed every three hours, has a gold-embossed Spanish reredos behind the altar. A silver monstrance on the altar holds a consecrated host, inviting contemplation. It is in this chapel where I am sitting in a pew, to pray before the Blessed Sacrament. The interior warmth of the building and the silence create a spiritual cocoon. This is consoling serenity. Suddenly, a blast of wind shakes the walls of the chapel.

The Santa Ana winds have begun. I had heard they were predicted. At certain times of the year, especially in autumn and winter, high pressure in the Great Basin creates these hot, dry winds that blow through the narrow mountain passes, gaining velocity as they sqeeze through the canyons and over flat land toward the Pacific Ocean. In the Santa Barbara area, these winds hit over forty miles per hour. On this day, the wind is not yet that strong, but there is a wild feeling that comes with it, prickly skin, dry throat, and a rush of energy that you feel in your whole body. There are wild winds like this in the Mediterranean and the Sahara too; they affect animal behavior and humans can get a little crazy.

This wild wind today is drawing me outside to experience its power. The outside temperature has climbed about twenty degrees. I walk out the front door of the monastery toward a trail that I know. It drops about five-hundred feet into Rattlesnake Canyon—yes there are lots of rattlesnakes, and bear, mountain lions, deer, fox, and coyotes. It is winter so the snakes should be hibernating.

I walk down a steep staircase of natural stone which has been shaped by centuries of water draining off the mountain. Arriving at another trail, I turn right, heading uphill. It is a weekday and there will be few hikers on this trail. Walking under the shelter of ancient oaks and sycamore trees, there is some protection from the wind. These Santa Anas come in sudden, powerful gusts. Trees bend and the entire landscape is caught up in a frenzy. Blue jays and crows fly to cover. A bushy-tailed bobcat crosses the

---

3. Lane, *Backpacking with the Saints*, 224.

trail, chasing a rabbit—or they both could be running to shelter. At the curve of the trail I drop down a side path leading to a stream. A surprise: in the shelter of a grove of intertwined oaks, a waterfall tumbles over mossy boulders. The wind blesses me with the spray from the waterfall. Gaining in strength, the wind gusts shake manzanita and sagebrush and the trees above groan, branches crash to the ground. I imagine the warm, protective monastery above me, where there will be strong coffee, and fresh bread. But awe and wonder at the power of nature holds me planted here by the water-fall, under the umbrella of oaks and sycamore. A break in the wind allows me to climb back up the stone staircase, but mid-way the wind returns with a vengeance, blinding me with clouds of dust, as I stagger slowly upward toward the sheltering walls of Mount Calvary. The natural vegetation on this mountainside can be the fastest-burning in the world. Winds like this create explosive fire danger.

And in November 2008, a horrific firestorm burned the monastery to the ground.

Perhaps a visual litmus test of our fear of wild places is the movie based on the popular book *Wild: Lost to Found on the Pacific Crest Trail*, by Cheryle Strayed. Wild places can purge the soul from dark events of the past. Walking through vast nature-space can wake us to the present moment of wonder and amazement, conjuring hope and peace and joy. The immense popularity of the book and movie may point to our innate desire to walk in the wild. Deep within our unconscious may be a vestigal memory of our primal ancestors and their holy communion with nature, where both animate and inanimate creation was filled with spirit presences. Many Native Americans have not lost this spiritual connection with the wild places.

As I channel-surf through the Weather Channel, the Discovery Channel, and PBS, a stream of disturbing images present back-to-nature scenarios in Alaska, Patagonia, and the Brazilian jungle. Terrifying scenes reveal the lives of alligators, rattlesnakes, mountain lions and wolves and our precarious relationship with them. Children and young people who see these programs have every reason to be afraid, to be very afraid of the natural world.

But if our deepest longing is connection with the sacred, the holy, the history of world spiritualities reminds us that to journey out there in nature, into the wild places, will stimulate an inner journey that can be life-changing.

Psychiatrist and spiritual writer Dr. Gerald G. May wrestled with his own fears about wild Nature. For Dr. May, walking and living in nature freed him from mental agendas and conflicts. Nature pulled him into the present moment. He found a wisdom and power out there in the empty spaces:

> Thus I learned about fear. The basic lesson is this. Fear is not an enemy, but a friend. Fear is something good, something alive, alert, and wild in us. Fear may be a response to danger, but fear itself is not dangerous. On the contrary, it is nothing other than life-spirit standing on its toes right here, right now with clear attention, sharp senses, ready body, flared nostrils, bristled hair, poised muscles, pumping heart, clean breath.
>
> The immense gratitude I experienced when I was most afraid was for feeling so incredibly alive. In untamed fear there is a profound sense of something that is me going through the experience. It is personhood without definition, identity without identification, selfhood without attributes. And it has an immense steadiness to it, an almost eternal quality. Here is this life, this being that is deeply myself, having this experience, being in it as I have been through every moment of the past, as I will be in every moment to come, no matter what. In this strange way, fear brought me an ultimate reassurance.[4]

In my desert journeys, the fears that enveloped me were not out there in Nature, but the anxieties and dread in my mental backpack. Such a heavy backpack! Will Erik be okay this week? Will I find enough money to keep the childcare center open? Will my cancer return? What I found in nature was a sensual backdrop for the revealing of the holy, God reaching out to me, that here in this desert place, just as at home with my family and work, I am loved.

Gerald May concludes:

> . . . what the Source of the All constantly yearns for: that each one of us will know without a doubt that we are loved, and that we are intimately, irrevocably part of the endless creation of love, and that we will join, with full freedom and consciousness, the joyous creativity that is Nature, that is Wildness, that is Wilderness, that is Everything.[5]

4. May, *Wisdom of Wilderness*, 46–47.
5. May, *Wisdom of Wilderness*, 190.

Chapter Nineteen

If You Read Only This, Read This. . .

Some people, in order to discover God, read books. But there is a
great book: the very appearance of created things. Look above you!
Look below you! Note it; read it. God, who you want to discover,
never wrote that book with ink; instead, He set before your eyes the
things that He had made. Can you ask for a louder voice than that?

—Augustine of Hippo[1]

He will accordingly feel that he has been led in a remarkably deep
and vast wilderness, unattainable by any human creature, into an
immense, unbounded desert, the more delightful, savorous, and loving, the deeper, vaster, and more solitary it is.

—John of the Cross[2]

The desert fathers and mothers are calling you into the desert.

Retreats in desert landscapes have renewed my awareness of being
God's beloved, and made me feel gratitude for the graces that have brought
me thus far. In contemplation, I close my eyes, breathe easily, and return
to those encounters with Jesus, a helpful prelude to inviting the Lord to be
present with me here and now.

1. Bourke, *Essential Augustine*, 123.
2. John of the Cross, *Collected Works*, 370.

Do you sense a desire to respond to God's invitation to come into desert places, in silence and solitude, to meet the Lord again—for the first time? How to do this? It is hard for us men to give ourselves permission to make a retreat because our lives can be rigidly tied to our professional calendars. We pencil it in as a good idea for some day. Some day never seems to happen.

Encouragement will come from outside ourselves. After I return from a retreat, my family says they see the peace of God in me. My parishioners have told me I am more present and attentive, and they appreciate how I weave the desert into sermons. Lutheran and Episcopal bishops encourage congregations to include time for retreats in a new pastor's letter of agreement. With issues of clergy misconduct, burn-out, conflict within congregations, diocesan and synod leaderships affirm retreats and spiritual direction as pro-active resources for clergy wellness. If clergy model self-care, this can encourage men in their congregations to see that retreats can bring solace and healing for their own souls.

At first, it was hard for me to justify time away from parish and family demands. The Spirit's nudging, through Sister Jeanne Fallon's and my wife's encouragement, started me off. After that, retreats in Advent and Lent, traditional seasons for reflection before Christmas and Easter, became the norm for me. My congregation anticipated my journeys in desert spaces with the Lord.

Some people tell me the desert is a monotonous space of sand and sagebrush that they endure on the way to Las Vegas or Phoenix, Arizona. That prejudice can change once you have had your feet on the desert ground, experiencing the desolate beauty and mysterious life that is there.

Between October and April is the best time for a retreat in the deserts of the Southwest. Two more men died in Death Valley last month, hiking in 120°F summer heat. You must go at the right time.

Where to go? Consider a place that has a story or unusual geology that intrigues you. Research that location so that when you arrive, you can search out remnants of history. Topographic maps will help you find the site. There are several map apps you can load on your cell phone to track your location as you follow a trail. But do not trust cell phone services to be always active. Desert hiking books share detailed advice for your preparations. I would emphasize lots of water, good hiking shoes and service your car before a desert trip. I leave word at home about my planned itinerary and when I go off into the desert, I leave a note inside by car with the time and day I departed and when I intend to return.

Not counting travel time, you will need at least three full days for a desert retreat. On the first day, as I walk a sandy trail through sagebrush and creosote, the busy mind is active, residual thoughts about things undone or things yet to do, distracting voices: what are you doing here? The first feelings of solitude and silence will help you focus on the landscape. I use *Animal Tracks: A Folding Pocket Guide to the Tracks and Signs of Familiar North American Species,* attempting to read the story of the tracks: rabbit prints and something larger following. Is there a story here? I have another card that identifies native plants and their medicinal uses.[3] We are walking through nature's pharmacy.

I chose a site for walking and meditation within two miles of a well-traveled road. I stay in a local motel for a good night's rest. Some will prefer camping in order to be closer to the landscape, nature, and the night sky.

The second and third day, when I have detoxed from the busy life, native instinct comes alive with the cold, dry, spicy scent of a desert morning. Eyes adjust to seeing long distances. Without the numbing background-buzz of city life, I can hear a kangaroo rat burrowing into a dune.

My friend Belden Lane, Professor of Spirituality at Saint Louis University, has a helpful suggestion: put into your backpack readings from a favorite saint or the desert fathers and mothers. I have brought with me *The Desert Fathers,* translated by Helen Waddell, and *The Wisdom of the Desert* by Thomas Merton. Belden Lane tells us:

> Taking a saint along on the trail, therefore, isn't an intellectual exercise. It's more like hiking with a Zen master, having someone to slap me upside the head as may be required. The words of the saints aren't meant to absorb me in thoughtful insight. More often than not, they stop thought altogether. 'Pay attention to what's going on around (and within) you. . . right now!' That's what they invariably insist. So, I seldom spend much time poring over a book in the wilderness. I graze, like bighorn sheep making their way over a rocky crag. I ponder lines I've underlined in a previous reading. I let the words sink in. Poetry is usually the best choice. A single saying of the Desert Fathers and Mothers can be more than enough.[4]

---

3. Kavanaugh, *Southwest Desert Plants.*

4. Lane, *Backpacking with the Saints,* xiv.

Sitting on a granite boulder in the shade of a piñon tree, for Morning Prayer I read aloud psalms from the breviary.

The sun rising out of Death Valley warms the back of my jacket. Gusts of wind scatter sand and dust. I cover my eyes to avoid the grit, but when I open them, the sacred words seem to have conjured a horned toad waddling toward my boots. Covered with spikes, its camouflaged body would be invisible if I had not noticed a suggestion of movement. I hold my breath as if it is telling me, "Don't move. Be still. This is the place to be right now. Listen!"

I sit in untimed silence, heart welling up with gratitude. A surge of joy enshrouds me, my throat tightens as I try to hold back tears. I fight this powerful feeling that possesses me, and then I let go to a shaking, sobbing body. At last, calm breathing returns. The horned toad gives an Amen and darts like a flash into a thicket of rabbit brush.

Years ago, I led a weekend retreat for six men from my Santa Ana parish to the desert spaces of the Eastern Sierra. We walked together through the ruins of a remote 1860s mining town and experienced several hours of solitary silence in the Alabama Hills. Meals together, the long drive and hiking on faint trails through sagebrush fostered a sense of kinship in the group.

We enter the desert, this numinous landscape, to walk with the Lord as God's beloved. Showing up is enough. Silence, solitude, and surprising encounters with desert life, releasing infusions of the Spirit can be like the snow, water and sun penetrating crevices in hard, granite rock.

You and I cannot be the same after being in the desert.

Bibliography

Abbey, Edward. *The Best of Edward Abbey*. San Francisco: Sierra Club, 1984.

Akpinar, Snjezana. "Hospitality in Islam." *Religion East and West: The Journal of the Institute for World Religions* (2007): 23.

Alcoholics Anonymous: The Big Book. New York: Alcoholics Anonymous World Services, 2002.

Alles, Gregory D., ed. *Autobiographical and Social Essays*. New York: de Gruyter, 1996.

Augustine of Hippo. *Confessions*. Edited by David Vincent Meconi. Translated by Maria Boulding. Chicago: Ignatius, 2012.

Barry, William A., and William J. Connolly. *The Practice of Spiritual Direction*. New York: HarperOne, 2009.

Bonhoeffer, Dietrich. *The Cost of Discipleship*. London: SCM, 2015.

Book of Common Prayer. New York: Church Publishing, 1979.

Bourke, Vernon, trans. *The Essential Augustine*, Cambridge, MA: Hackett, 1974.

Campbell, Joseph. *Hero With a Thousand Faces*. Princeton, NJ: Princeton University Press, 1973.

Chang, Kenneth. "Secrets of the Singing Sand Dunes." *New York Times*, July 25, 2006. https://www.nytimes.com/2006/07/25/science/25find.html.

Chesterton, G. K. *The Collected Works of G. K. Chesterton*. Chicago: Ignatius, 1994.

Chittister, Joan. *Called to Question: A Spiritual Memory*. London: Sheed and Ward, 2004.

Christian Prayer: The Liturgy of the Hours. New York: Catholic Book, 1976.

Conway, John S. "The 'Stasi' and the Churches: Between Coercion and Compromise in East German Protestantism, 1949–89." *A Journal of Church and State* 36.4 (1994): 725–45.

Dart, Ron. *Hermann Hesse: Phoenix Arising*. Abbotsford, BC: Paideia, 2019.

de Mello, Anthony. *Wellsprings: A Book of Spiritual Exercises*. Baltimore, MD: Image, 2013.

De Waal, Esther. *A Life-Giving Way: A Commentary on the Rule of St. Benedict*. Norwich, UK: Canterbury, 2006.

Eldredge, John. *Wild at Heart: Discovering Secrets of a Man's Soul*. New York: Thomas Nelson, 2006.

Ellsberg, Robert, ed. *Carlo Carretto: Selected Writings*. Maryknoll: NY, 2007.

Faith at Marquette, https://www.marquette.edu/faith/examen-of-consciousness.php

Ferguson, Gary. "The Great Fear of the Great Outdoors." *Los Angeles Times*, December 21, 2014.

Fox, Matthew, ed. *Hildegard of Bingen's Book of Divine Works, with Letters and Songs*. Santa Fe, NM: Bear & Company, 1987.

Francaviglia, Richard V. *Believing in Places: A Spiritual Geography of the Great Basin.* Reno, NV: University of Nevada Press, 2003.

Fry, Timothy, ed. *RB 1980: The Rule of St. Benedict in English.* Collegeville, MN: Liturgical, 1981.

Galarreta, Lori. "One Man's Mission to Keep Aztecs' Ancient Language Alive." Pasadena, CA: KPCC Public Radio. https://www.kqed.org/news/11352009/one-mans-mission-to-keep-aztecs-ancient-language-alive.

Gallagher, Timothy. *The Examen Prayer: Ignatian Wisdom for Our Lives Today.* New York: Crossroad, 2006.

———. *A Layman's Guide to the Liturgy of the Hours: How the Prayers of the Church Can Change Your Life.* Irondale, AL: EWTN, 2019.

Goldberg, Nathan. *Passover Haggadah.* Brooklyn, NY: KTAV, 2021.

Grey, Zane. *Stairs of Sand: A Western Story.* New York: Skyhorse, 2017.

Grinnell, Joseph. "Birds are Rediscovering Owens Lake," Steve Hymon, *Los Angeles Times,* January 21, 2002.

Hall, G. Stanley. *Youth: Its Education, Regimen and Hygiene.* London: Aeterna, 2020.

Harris, Tod W. "The Revolutionary Church? The Role of East German Protestants Amid Political Change." *Occasional Papers on Religion in Eastern Europe* 12.6.2 (1992): https://digitalcommons.georgefox.edu/ree/vol12/iss6/2.

Hogue, Lawrence. *The Wild and Lonely Places: Journeys in a Desert Landscape.* Washington, DC: Island, 2000.

Hopler, Whitney. *Saint Francis of Assisi and His Sermon to Birds, Learn Religion.* August 27, 2020, https://www.learnreligions.com/saint-francis-assisi-sermon-to-birds-124321

Hung, Steve. "Tom Hamilton, PHS Icon, Dies of Cancer." *Pasadena Star News,* March 15, 2004.

Jasper, David. *The Sacred Desert.* Hoboken, NJ: Wiley-Blackwell, 2004.

John of the Cross. *The Collected Works.* Translated by Kieran Kavanaugh. Nashville, TN: Thomas Nelson, 1966.

John of the Cross. *Ascent of Mount Carmel.* Translated by Kieran Kavanaugh. London: SPCK, 1987.

Johnston, William. *Silent Music.* New York: Harper and Row, 1974.

Jung, C. G. *Collected Works of C. G. Young, Volume 9, Part I.* Edited by Gerhard Adler and R.F.C. Hull. Princeton, NJ: Princeton University Press, 1981.

Kappel-Smith, Diana. *Desert Time: A Journey Through the American Southwest.* Tucson, AZ: The University of Arizona Press, 1992.

Karelius, Brad. *Desert Spirit Places: The Sacred Southwest.* Eugene, OR: Wipf and Stock, 2019.

———. *Encounters with the World's Religions; The Numinous on Highway 395.* Eugene, OR: Wipf and Stock, 2015.

———. *The Spirit in the Desert: Sacred Sites in the Owens Valley.* Laguna Niguel, CA: Desert Spirit, 2009.

Kavanaugh, James. *Animal Tracks: A Folding Pocket Guide to the Tracks and Signs of Familiar North American Species.* Tampa, FL: Waterford, 2018.

———. *Southwest Desert Plants: A Folding Pocket Guide to Familiar Plants.* Tampa, FL: Waterford, 2018.

Kavanaugh, Kieran. *The Wisdom of Teresa: Selections from the Interior Castle.* Mahwah, NJ: Paulist, 1997.

Kearney, Richard. *Hosting the Stranger: Between Religions.* London: Continuum, 2011.

Kingsolver, Barbara, *Small Wonder*. New York: HarperCollins, 2002.

Kosloski, Phillip. "A Beginner's Guide to Praying the Liturgy of the Hours." http://www.philipkosloski.com/a-beginners-guide-to-praying-the-liturgy-of-the-hours/

Krutch, Joseph Wood. *The Desert Year*. Tucson, AZ: University of Arizona Press, 1952.

Kummer, Armin M. *Men, Spirituality and Gender-specific Biblical Hermeneutics*. Leuven, Belgium: Peeters, 2019.

Kurdek, Lawrence. "The Ties That Unbind." *Psychology Today*. January 1, 2000.

Kushner, Harold S. *Conquering Fear: Living Boldly in an Uncertain World*. New York: Knopf, 2009.

Lane, Belden C. *Backpacking with the Saints: Wilderness Hiking as Spiritual Practice*. Oxford: Oxford University Press, 2015.

———. *Landscapes of the Sacred: Geography and Narrative in American Spirituality*. Baltimore, MD: Johns Hopkins University Press, 2001.

———. *The Great Conversation: Nature and the Care of the Soul*. Oxford: Oxford University Press, 2019.

Langley, Christopher. "Perry Cardoza's Land Art Project Breaks Ground in the Owens Valley," February 3, 2016. https://www.kcet.org/shows/artbound/perry-cardozas-land-art-project-breaks-ground-in-the-owens-valley

Lewis, C. S. *The Problem of Pain*. New York: HarperCollins, 2009.

Lopardo, Steve, *Our Best Advice*. Privately published.

Los Angeles Department of Water and Power. *Owens Lake Trails: A Public Access, Education and Recreation Project of the LADWP Owens Lake Dust Mitigation Program*.

Lowney, Chris. *Heroic Leadership: Best Practice from a 450-Year-Old Company That Changed the World*. Chicago: Loyola, 2005.

Loyola, St. Ignatius. *The Spiritual Exercises of St. Ignatius Loyola*. Charlotte, NC: Tan, 1999.

Marcarios of Corinth. *Philokalia Volume II*. Edited by St. Nicodemus the Hagiorite. Belmont, MA: Institute for Byzantine and Modern Greek Studies, 2009.

Martin, James. *Learning to Pray: A Guide for Everyone*. New York: HarperOne, 2021.

———. *My Life with the Saints*. Chicago: Loyola, 2010.

———. *The Jesuit Guide to (Almost) Everything: A Spirituality for Real Life*. New York: HarperOne, 2010.

May, Gerald G. *Wisdom of Wilderness: Experiencing the Healing Power of Nature*. New York: HarperCollins, 2006.

McDermatt, Jim. "Men are Struggling with their Spirituality." *America Magazine*, May 8, 2019.

Merton, Thomas. *Conjectures of a Guilty Bystander*. New York: Image, 2009.

———. *Contemplative Prayer*. New York: Doubleday, 1989.

———. *No Man Is an Island*. Boulder, CO: Shambhala, 2005.

———. *Seven Storey Mountain*. New York: Harcourt, Brace, 1948.

———. *The Intimate Merton: His Life from his Journals*. New York: HarperOne, 2001.

———. *The Wisdom of the Desert*. New York: New Directions, 1960.

Mundy, Linus. *A Retreat with Desert Mystics*. Cincinnati, OH: St. Anthony Messenger, 1989.

Neubert, Ehrhart. *Geschichte de Opposition in der DDR 1949–1989*. Berlin: Christoph Links, 1997.

Nouwen, Henri. *Spiritual Direction: Wisdom for the Long Walk of Faith*. New York: HarperOne, 2006.

———. *Bread for the Journey: A Daybook of Wisdom and Faith.* New York: HarperOne, 2006.

——— . *Inner Voice of Love.* New York: Image, 2010.

Otto, Rudolf. *The Idea of the Holy: An Inquiry into the Non-rational Factor in the Idea of the Divine and its Relation to the Rational.* Oxford: Oxford University Press, 1958.

Patterson, Bobbi. *Building Resilience through Contemplative Practice.* Milton Park, UK: Routledge, 2019.

Pennington, Basil. *Centering Prayer.* New York: Doubleday, 1980.

Pew Research Center. "Q & A: Why are Women Generally More Religious than Men?" March 23, 2016. https://www.pewresearch.org/fact-tank/2016/03/23/qa-why-are-women-generally-more-religious-than-men/

Pew Research Center. "The Gender Gap in Religion Around the World." March 22, 2016. https://www.pewforum.org/2016/03/22/the-gender-gap-in-religion-around-the-world/

Plotkin, Bill. *Soulcraft: Crossing into the Mysteries of Nature and Psyche.* Novato, CA: New World Library, 2003.

Poulain, August. *Graces of Interior Prayer.* Gilbert, AZ: Caritas, 2016.

Presto, Greg. "Birdwatching Is an Easy Way to Practice Mindfulness." https://www.vice.com/en/article/evq457/birdwatching-mindfulness-meditation-benefits-birding

Rahner, Karl. *The Need and Blessing of Prayer.* Collegeville, MN: Liturgical, 1997.

Rohr, Richard. *Falling Upward: A Spirituality for the Two Halves of Life.* San Francisco, CA: Jossey-Bass, 2011.

———. *From Wild Man to Wise Man: Reflections on Male Spirituality.* Cincinnati, OH: Saint Anthony Messenger, 2005.

———. *Nature as a Mirror of God*, March 12, 2018. https://cac.org/nature-as-a-mirror-of-god-2018–03–12/.

Rolheiser, Ron. "A Meditation on Joy," https://ronrolheiser.com/a-meditation-on-joy/#.YS_GhY5KjE4.

———. "Contemplative Prayer," https://ronrolheiser.com/contemplative-prayer/#.YlWL1ZPML0.

———. *The Holy Longing.* New York: Doubleday, 1999.

———. "Home—The Place from which to Understand." https://ronrolheiser.com/home-the-place-from-which-to-understand/#.YPCBhuhKjE4

———. *Prayer: Our Deepest Longing.* Cincinnati, OH: Franciscan Media, 2013.

———. "Resting in God's Presence." https://www.franciscanmedia.org/franciscan-spirit-blog/resting-in-gods-presence.

———. "Sustaining A Prayer Life." https://ronrolheiser.com/sustaining-a-prayer-life/#.YJwu4KhKjE4

Sacks, Jonathan. *A Sense of History.* https://rabbisacks.org/ki-tavo-a-sense-of-history/

Sagahun, Louis. "Owens Lake." *Los Angeles Times*, April 28, 2018.

San Roman, Gabriel. "For the Past 20 Years a Santa Ana Man has kept the Language of the Aztecs Alive." *OC Weekly*, December 1, 2016.

Schulman, Miriam, and Amal Barkouki-Winter. "The Extra Mile: The Ancient Virtue of Hospitality Imposes Duties on Host and Guest." *Issues in Ethics* 2.1 (2000): https://www.scu.edu/mcae/publications/iie/v11n1/hospitality.html.

Shea, John. *Starlight.* Chicago: ACTA, 2006.

Sheldrake, Philip. *Living Between Worlds.* London: Darton, Longman & Todd, 1995.

"Singing Sand Dunes." *National Geographic*. Youtube video. 5:12. https://www.youtube.com/watch?v=4mbypyJjqhk.

Smith, Steven. *Walking Meditation*. https://www.contemplativemind.org/practices/tree/walking-meditation.

Strayed, Cheryle. *Wild: Lost to Found on the Pacific Crest Trail*. Waterville, ME: Thorndike, 2013.

Taylor, Charles. *A Secular Age*. Cambridge, MA: Harvard University Press, 2007.

Thompson, Hunter S. "The 'Hashbury' is the Capital of the Hippies." *New York Times*, May 14, 1967.

Trzebiatowska, Marta and Steve Bruce. *Why Are Women More Religious than Men?* Oxford: Oxford University Press, 2012.

U. S Department of Health and Human Services. National Vital Statistics. Series 21–38. July, 1981.

Van Dyke, John. *The Desert*. Sydney, Australia: Wentworth, 2019.

Vazquez, David. *La Voz de Tenochtitlan: La Lengua Azteca* (The Voice of Tenochtitlan: The Aztec Language). Self-published, 1993.

Waddell, Helen, trans. *The Desert Fathers*. New York: Vintage Books, 1998.

Ward, Benedicta. *The Sayings of the Desert Fathers: The Alphabetical Collection*. Cistercian Studies. Mexico City, Buena, 2006.

Whyte, David. *The Three Marriages*. New York: Riverhead, 2009.

Wild, Peter, ed. *The Desert Reader*. Salt Lake City, UT: University of Utah Press, 1991.

Index